CW00972040

BISON
BOOKS

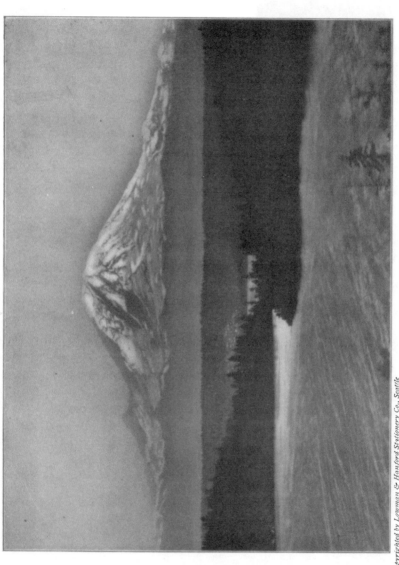

TAKHOMA, "THE WHITE MOUNTAIN," AS SEEN FROM SEATTLE. (MOUNT RAINIER)

MYTHS AND LEGENDS
OF THE
PACIFIC NORTHWEST

SELECTED BY KATHARINE BERRY JUDSON

Introduction to the Bison Books Edition
by Jay Miller

University of Nebraska Press
Lincoln and London

Introduction © 1997 by the University of Nebraska Press
Manufactured in the United States of America

⊛ The paper in this book meets the minimum requirements of American National Standard for Information Sciences—Permanence of Paper
for Printed Library Materials, ANSI Z39.48-1984.

First Bison Books printing: 1997
Most recent printing indicated by the last digit below:
10   9   8   7   6   5   4   3   2   1

Library of Congress Cataloging-in-Publication Data
Judson, Katharine Berry.
Myths and legends of the Pacific Northwest / Selected by Katharine
Berry Judson.
p.   cm.
Originally published: Chicago: A. C. McClurg, 1910.
Includes bibliographical references.
ISBN 0-8032-7595-1 (pbk.: alk. paper)
1. Indians of North America—Northwest Coast of North America—
Folklore.   2. Indian mythology—Northwest Coast of North America.
3. Legends—Northwest Coast of North America.   I. Title.
E78.N78J83   1997
398.2'089970795—dc21
96-39239   CIP

Reprinted from the original 1910 edition by A. C. McClurg & Co.,
Chicago.

INTRODUCTION

Jay Miller

This entertaining sampler brings together stories from all over Native North America. The majority are from northern California, where the Klamath, Shastan, and Pit Rivers (Atsugewi, Achomawi) still live. Only the Cowlitz, Klickitat, Yakima, and Okanogan are in Washington State, while the Tillamook and Modoc are in Oregon. The Chinook, including the Clatsop, occupied the lower Columbia River, the border between these two states.

Katharine Berry Judson, the compiler, was born in Poughkeepsie, New York, and received a B.A. from Cornell in 1904, before earning a librarianship degree in 1905 and an M.A. in history at the University of Washington in 1911. Between these dates, she was a librarian in Kalispell, Montana, for a year and then head of periodicals for the Seattle Public Library, where she assembled four collections of native stories.

As she explains, these stories were collected during her quest to find an "authentic" native version of the story of the bridge of the gods, a stone span across the Columbia that collapsed in punishment for some thwarted love. It is symptomatic of European attitudes toward Native Americans that she did not stop to realize that stone bridges were never a part of local native technology. Similarly, she treats all natives as though they lived in tipis, wore leather clothing, and called their women squaws. Such stereotypes are, of course, derogatory because they deny the complex richness of native life. In particular, photo captions calling attention to grave goods (facing page 77) or blaming the Whitman massacre solely on victimized Cayuse (facing page 103) are no longer acceptable.

1

Many tribal names have now been changed to accord with what people call themselves instead of how some outsider first wrote down a name for them. Thus, Nootka are again properly Nuchahnulth, Kwakiutl are Kwakwaka'wakw, Nez Perce are Numipu, Yakima are Yakama, and Puget Salish are Lushootseed.

In all, Washington and Oregon natives partook of four different lifeways. Called "culture areas" by scholars, each of these ways of living was an intermesh of climate, local foods, social institutions, and beliefs. The shores of the Pacific Ocean from Alaska to California is known as the Northwest Coast, with salmon, canoes, cedar plank longhouses, and masked feasting. Across the Cascade Mountains to the east is the Plateau, with salmon, tubers, rush mat longhouses, and winter enactments of encounters with spirit immortals. Further to the east is the Plains, famous for bison, small skin tipis, and elaborately costumed dances. However, the most famous feature of the Plains, its horse-riding warriors, lasted only two centuries after Spanish herds spread throughout American grasslands in the late 1600s. During that time, the attraction of horse, tall tipis, and fancy trade goods spread Plains features across the continent so that all natives are now expected, unfortunately, to wear a feather headdress. Further to the south was native California, whose northern province was noted for salmon, acorns, plank houses for families, plank sweathouses for men, and the display of exotic goods, valued for their beauty and rarity, such as red woodpecker scalps, albino deerskins, and colorful obsidian blades a yard long.

While this book includes a scattering of words that are attempts to render native languages, a nearly impossible task because of the severe limitations of the English alphabet, the majority of unusual terms come from "chinook jargon," a list of words adopted to encourage intertribal trading among native people visiting towns along the lower Columbia River. Taking simplified terms from local Chinook and from the Nootkan languages of the west coast of Vancouver Island, Judson added other words as needed. For example, *boston* became the designation for all Americans because many of the early ships sailed from that port and natives were primarily identified by their home towns. By contrast, English were *kinchachman,* from King George man.

Among the chinook terms in this collection are *Tyhee Sahale* (8), meaning Lord Above or God; *Tatoosh* (8), "breast(s), milk," not Thunderbird; *skookum* (40), "strong," especially a dangerous spirit; *tomanowos* (48), more often *tahmanowas,* from *tah* "spirit," meaning "spiritual, magical, supernatural, extraordinary"; *kloochman* (74), "woman, wife"; *ikta* (74), "thing, goods, package"; *hiaqua* (74), often *hiqua,* "dentalium, tusk shell money"; and *tum* (125), "heart, mind, soul, pulse, pounding," hence *tum-tum* "waterfall."

All of these stories clearly originated in native tellings, although they have been recast for an American audience. Among those features carrying a sense of native literature are the use of a pattern number, often five in these stories according to the Plateau manner; the role of mouse as go-between; and the firm conviction that animals are people too. Regional features of the Northwest are the psychotic character of Mrs. Grizzly, Crane using his leg as a bridge, mention of an all-copper canoe, and the many adventures of Coyote.

So much of the understanding of these stories depends on context and immersion in community life that readers can miss the motivation for an act. For example, the great humor in the story about Kemush's robe is that he jumps ahead of himself and literally counts his chickens well before they are hatched. Tearing up his rabbit blanket before he had even aimed at a lynx was very poor planning, as was attacking an antelope without a weapon at the ready. Moreover, appeals to fashion were not the way to slow down an animal fleeing for its life.

Throughout the Northwest, both twins and salmon (who are often called by the same exact word) express in a poetic sense the two sides of things, such as the life and death played out each year by the returning fish, the growing crop, and the very twoness of humans born at the same time and place. So serious was and is this connection, however, that the parents of newborn twins could not go near water for a year until the babies had become more human. Thereafter, as long as they lived, twins had a special relationship with salmon and could summon them to ease a threat of starvation.

This collection also hints at greater tribal epics. The first story about the theft of daylight from Gull by Raven is but a flicker of the great epic of how Raven stole the sun, moon, and stars from the Grandfather at the Head of the Nass River. When, after his hard work, those fishing in the dark refused to give Raven any of their catch, he threw open the box so that a blinding flash transformed the entire world, changing beings without definite form into modern species, places, and sounds. Only the frogs remained close to their primordial shape, shifting throughout their lives from wiggling tadpole to lumpy hopper.

Similarly, when Coyote made Spokane Falls (118) or released salmon from a trap owned by Skookum women at the mouth of the Klamath River, these were incidents of a longer epic. Throughout the Plateau, people tell of how Coyote liberated salmon from a trap belonging to seabirds, and brought these fish up the length of the Columbia River. The size and quality of the salmon left in each tributary depended on the beauty of the "wife" Coyote visited in the nearest town (Miller 1992:93–98). The wonderfully ironic twist to the account published herein is that Coyote says he is looking for the "key" to the trap dam, a thoroughly foreign notion.

While this collection ends with a tale of Coyote's death, do not believe it. Coyote never dies, although he goes to sleep for a very long time until a relative such as Red or Silver Fox steps over the last shred of his bone and he immediately jumps up, as whole and guileless as ever.

The most problematic feature of the entire book is Judson's preface. She begins with a lone native and his few tools, instead of, more correctly, with a vibrant and living world populated by communities of beings, some human, some plant, some animal, some localized, and some immortal. Each of these beings was a person, often with an essential human form under the cloak of their species. Over all, there was indeed a "benevolent deity," variously known as Heaven, Creator, or Lord Above, who took much more interest in leading families and so was infrequently mentioned in popular accounts. In their dealings with all of these beings, natives were neither fearful nor contrite since the animated world also shared their emotional sense of purpose. Their world was humane, based on dignity and responsiveness (not on cunning). After generations of observation, accumulated wisdom was passed on, often in stories. Thus, Loowit was given fire, as confirmed each century by the volcanic eruption of Mount Saint Helens, most recently on 18 May 1980.

In all, the tales represent a distillation of tribal memory, apt negative examples to teach native children what not to do, and a personification of environmental wisdom.

The theft of fire, destruction of primordial monsters, implanting of waterfalls, and first instruction in useful arts are details along the way of "marking the landscape to prepare the world for human arrival." The connectedness of everything was illustrated by stories of how things came to be as they are. Particular hills, streams, food sources, and events like earthquakes are explained by human-like actions by Animal People at the beginning. These people were shape shifters, shimmering between humans, species, space, and time. Often in the Northwest, only the immortals kept their shimmering character after the world changed forever, sometimes by capsizing just like a canoe.

Along some rivers, ancestral beings arrive by canoe, settling towns along that route, much as certain Greek city states regarded their founder as a named crew member of Odysseus (Ulysses) or of Jason and the Argonauts. Other places traced their origins to the acts of Hercules, leaving lasting features like any other tribal culture hero. Like Prometheus stealing fire, so the shimmering immortals of American belief also acted out of compassion for human needs.

Among the people at the beginning were some who later became mountains. The peak south of Seattle, near the city of Tacoma, was named by Captain George Vancouver for British Admiral Peter Rainier (jokingly spelled rainy-er because of the climate), again in the distinctly European notion that each mountain should have its own name. Local natives also had several names for different kinds of mountains, both separately and together. For those few, such as Rainier or Baker, which were permanently snow capped, the term $taq^w oba$ is used, making specific reference to frozen fresh water.

INTRODUCTION

Over a century ago, Lushootseed shifted some sounds from /m/ to /b/ and from /n/ to /d/, which explains why early settlers spelled this word Takoma. During much of that time, writers uninformed about this Salishan language have sought highly romantic translations instead of the ecological precision of the native term.

Forbidden during summer when much work had to be done, stories were told on long, rainy winter nights. Alternating serious and comic incidents, storytellers entertained an audience of all ages. For the older members, moreover, stories were comfortable, familiar ways to justify customs and consensus. For the curious, they also hid rich symbols, such as a volcano disguised as a woman, star orbits treated as dances, or long abandoned towns returned to life. By pondering these deeper significances, bright minds explored ancient understandings. Lastly, stories allowed everyone to agree on how they should act and how things should be done. By carefully selecting and retelling this impressive range of stories, Judson enables the reader to share native concerns in many times, places, and dimensions.

REFERENCES

Bates, Dawn, Thom Hess, and Vi Hilbert
   1994   *Lushootseed Dictionary.* Seattle: University of Washington Press.
Gill, John
   1909   *Dictionary of the Chinook Jargon.* Portland OR: J. K. Gill Company.
Miller, Jay
   1992   *Earthmaker: Tribal Stories from Native North America.* New York: Putnam Perigree.

PREFACE

IN the days of the first grandfather, when the
earth was young, the Indian, armed only with
stone knife, stone hatchet, and bows and arrows,
found himself confronted with the work of Some
One far greater and stronger than himself. This
Power, or Powers, for there came to be many of
them, had uplifted snowy mountain peaks, had cut
deep cañons through the solid rock, had carved out
mountain passes, and had blocked the passage of
mighty rivers by great rocks and bowlders. These
Powers were strong and brutal. They had enormous
strength and men of only human size were their
prey, as helpless as " flybug " under the heel of the
Indian. Tatoosh, the Thunder Bird who lived in
the sky, was one of these Powers. He shook the
mountains with the flapping of his wings. The
flashing of his eye was the lightning. He caught
great whales instead of salmon for food. Only by
crumbling a rock into powder so small that he could
not even see it, could he secure a piece small enough

for the Indian to use as a salmon spear. Because Tatoosh is so terrible and the enemy of red men, his picture is painted and carved on their houses, their canoes, and canoe paddles, indeed everywhere, to soften his anger. Often Tatoosh, as shown in the photograph of the Chilcat blanket, is represented by a single eye — the terrible eye that flashes fire. There is no beneficent deity among these Indians of the Northwest. Sahale does not represent the same idea as that of Manitou, the Great Spirit, among the eastern Indians. Yet Tyhee Sahale, along the Columbia River, and Old Man Above, among the California Indians, represent the clearest idea of a single governing spirit living in the sky. But they are not sure of his friendship. Among most of the tribes, on the other hand, there is an utter lack of any friendly deity, as among the Blackfeet, of Montana, with whom Old Man is simply a trickster, half human, who nearly always gets the worst of it in his encounters with Coyote.

So the Indian felt powerless against the gods who made the earth — the forces of nature which he could not understand. In his helplessness, he was influenced by the animal life he saw about him. In the tragedies of the forest he saw the weaker, smaller creatures escape the larger ones only by cunning. So must he by cunning escape the anger of the gods. The crafty animals became his earth gods and in time his helpers. Coyote, the weakest but craftiest of all the animals, became, on the coast, " the chief of all the animals." Fox ranked second.

The adventures of Coyote, like those of Yehl, the Raven, of Alaska, are " so many that no one could tell them all." Professor F. S. Lyman, however, groups them around three or four main heads: the theft of fire, the destruction of monsters, the making of waterfalls, and the teaching of useful arts to the Indians.

Now the animal people lived before the days of the first grandfather, long, long ago, when the sun was new and no larger than a star, when the earth was young, and the tall firs of the forest no larger than an arrow. These were the days of the animal people. People had not " come out " yet.

" Then Coyote said, ' I want it to be foggy.' So it was foggy. Then all the people came out. No one saw them come. Coyote said, ' I want the sun to shine.' So the sun shone and the fog drifted away. Then the people were there. No one saw them come out."

But with people there must needs be fire.

Where did fire come from ? This question which

has puzzled every tribe and nation, each has solved in its own way. With the Greek, as with the red man, fire was first only on a mountain top, carefully guarded as a precious possession, and to be secured only by theft. Among the Greeks, a god took pity on shivering, unhappy mortals. Among the Indians it was an animal god, usually Coyote, who stole it. With both peoples, mountains were the homes of supernatural beings. A comparison between Greek and red men may seem far-fetched to Greek scholars, yet there is a striking similarity, and it is one which is of peculiar interest to those who live within full view of the wonderful "White Mountain." Olympus, rising above Homer's "sounding sea" on which rode the "black ships," was peopled with the immortal gods. Takhoma, lifting its snowy head above the waters of Whulge on which rode the frail Indian canoes, was the home of the dreaded tomanowos. With both peoples the mountains were sacred. Avalanches and volcanic eruptions on Takhoma were caused by the tomanowos and nothing could tempt the red man to climb high above the snow line. If encamped below it, the Indian, awakened in the darkness by the sound of falling ice and snow, started from his blanket and sang a dirge-like song to appease the wrath of the spirits. Takhoma was associated with mystery and danger. No red man dared risk the fate of the miser.

Indian nomenclature has been used entirely in this volume, since the myths, of course, date far back of the coming of the white man. In due time, it is believed, the Northwest will again come to use the beautiful Indian names instead of the commonplace ones given by the whites. There is no good reason why Kulshan, "The Great White Watcher," should be called by the prosaic name of Mount Baker. Still less reason is there for calling Takhoma, "The White Mountain," by the name of an English admiral (Rainier) who never saw the mountain and never came into the Northwest. Many Indian names, it is true, have been preserved, but the fate which the beautiful mountain peaks along the coast have suffered give reason for congratulation that Umatilla, "Wind-drifted Sands," escaped being called "Sand Hole," and that Chelan, "Beautiful Waters," is not on the map as "Long Lake."

The exact meaning of "Takhoma" is in dispute. It is given as "The White Mountain" and also as the "Fountain-breast of Milk-white Waters." As Indian nomenclature was governed by the most striking physical feature of the thing named, be it man or mountain, the simple directness of "The White

PREFACE

Mountain" seems to the writer to be more truly Indian. The most striking thing about Takhoma, as seen on any sunny day, is its intense whiteness. It is gloriously white, dazzling, as it lifts its head fifteen thousand feet from the sea level of the surrounding country into the deep blue sky. Therefore the more expressive interpretation has been preferred.

The basis on which these myths were selected necessarily excluded those which showed traces of the white man's religion or of the red man's coarseness. Relatively speaking, only a few myths could be selected. These were the creation myths, the origin of the races, the theft of fire, the salmon, and especially those connected with the physical features of the country, such as those of Takhoma, Shasta, the Columbia River, and the group of mountains of the bridge of the gods. The collection grew out of an effort to find, simply for personal amusement, a complete and authentic account of the legend of the bridge of the gods. It is one which is well known, yet I had difficulty in finding it, and the search revealed many quaint local myths that were practically inaccessible to the general reader.

No claim is made for original work in this volume, except with regard to the selection of the myths and the rewriting of several in which the Indian simplicity and directness had been destroyed by attempted witticisms, by philosophical remarks, or by wordy explanations. A consistent effort has been made to tell these stories as the Indians told them. Some of the legends, such as the " Duration of Life," " Old Grizzly and Old Antelope," and the " Robe of Kemush " are almost literal translations from the Indian, as recorded by government ethnologists. With regard to the use of the name " Kemush," it may be remarked incidentally that this is a popular and abbreviated form of the name " K'mutkmitch."

Neither is this volume intended to be a very serious or a learned one. It is, however, authentic. All myths for which a responsible authority could not be found have been rejected. The chief sources of information used, by permission, were the ethnological reports of the Government, of learned societies, and such publications as " The American Anthropologist " and " The Journal of American Folklore." The work of such ethnologists as Franz Boas, John R. Swanton, and Albert S. Gatschet has been freely used. Indebtedness is also acknowledged to Professor W. D. Lyman and Professor F. S. Lyman, to the work of Hubert Howe Bancroft, and to the writings of Louise McDermott, Alice C. Fletcher, Herbert J. Spinden, Roland B. Dixon, Mrs. R. S. Shackelford,

PREFACE

J. Owen Dorsey, and others. Acknowledgment for courtesies received is also due to the photographers, and to Lowman & Hanford, of Seattle, but especially to Major Lee Moorhouse, of Pendleton, Oregon.

K. B. J.

SEATTLE PUBLIC LIBRARY,
July 15, 1910.

TABLE OF CONTENTS

TABLE OF CONTENTS

ILLUSTRATIONS

ILLUSTRATIONS

MYTHS AND LEGENDS OF THE PACIFIC NORTHWEST

THE ORIGIN OF DAYLIGHT

Nanaimo modification
of the Thlingit legend

WHEN the earth was very new and young, it was dark and cold and gray. Even the stars were black. There was no light anywhere for Gull kept it in a small box which he guarded carefully. His cousin, Raven, was tired of the dark. He wished for the daylight. One day when Gull and Raven were out walking, Raven thought, "I wish Gull would run a thorn into his foot." Hardly had he thought so, when, in the darkness, Gull stepped on a thorn.

"*Sqenán!* My foot!" cried Gull.

"A thorn?" asked Raven. "Let me see it. I will take it out."

But it was so dark Raven could not see the thorn. He asked Gull to open the box and make it light. Gull opened it just a little way and the light was very faint.

Raven said, "You must give me more light."

Gull answered, "*Sqenán!*"

So Raven pretended not to see the thorn. Instead of pulling it out, he pushed it in deeper and deeper, saying, "You must give me more light."

"*Sqenán! sqenán!* My foot! my foot!" cried Gull. Raven pushed the thorn in deeper and deeper until Gull at last opened the box. That is the way the daylight came.

HOW SILVER-FOX CREATED THE WORLD

Hat Creek Indians
(Atsugewi)

IN the beginning there was nothing but water. Coyote and Silver-Fox lived above in the sky, where there was a world like this one. Silver-Fox was anxious to make things, but Coyote was opposed to this. Finally Silver-Fox got tired of Coyote and sent him one day to get wood. While he was gone, Silver-Fox took an arrow-flaker and made a hole in the upper world, and looked down on the sea below. When Coyote came back, Silver-Fox did not tell him about the hole he had made. Next day he sent Coyote off again for wood. While he was gone Silver-Fox thrust down the arrow-flaker and found that it reached to the water and down to the bottom of the water. So he climbed through the hole. As he came near the surface of the water, he made a little round island on which he stayed. When Coyote returned, he could not find Silver-Fox, and after hunting a long time, he began to feel remorseful. Finally he found the hole in the sky. He peeped through and saw Silver-Fox on his island, far, far below. He called to Silver-Fox he was sorry, and asked how to get down. Silver-Fox did not answer. Coyote said Silver-Fox ought not to treat him so badly; then Silver-Fox put up the arrow-flaker and Coyote came down.

But the island was very small, and there was not room enough for Coyote to stretch out. For some time they slept and when they awoke they were very hungry. For five days things continued this way, until at last Silver-Fox gave Coyote some sunflower seeds. He asked where they came from. Silver-Fox did not answer.

After five days more, Silver-Fox made the island a little larger so that Coyote could have room to stretch out. At last he went comfortably asleep. At once Silver-Fox got up, dressed himself finely, and then made a big sweat house. When it was all done, he woke Coyote, who was much surprised to see the sweat house. Silver-Fox told Coyote to sweep it out, to spread grass on the floor, and to go to sleep again. He did so, and Silver-Fox dressed up again. He put on a finely beaded shirt

"THERE WAS NO LIGHT ANYWHERE FOR GULL KEPT IT IN A SMALL BOX"

(Page 19)

MOUNT HOOD

Copyrighted by Kiser Photo. Co.

and leggings, and smoked and sang more. Then, going outside, he pushed with his foot, and stretched out the earth in all directions, first to the east, then to the north, then to the west, and last to the south. For five nights he repeated this, until the world became as large as it is to-day. Each day Silver-Fox told Coyote to run around the edge and see how large it was growing. At first Coyote could do this very quickly; but the last time he grew old and gray before he got back. Then Silver-Fox made trees and springs and fixed the world up nicely. He also made all kinds of animals, merely by thinking about them. These animals, however, were like people.

When the world was all made, Coyote asked what they were going to have for food. Silver-Fox did not reply. Coyote then said he thought there ought to be ten moons of winter in the year. Silver-Fox replied there would not be enough food for so long a winter. Coyote said it would be better not to have much food, that people could make soup out of dirt. Silver-Fox at first did not reply. Then Silver-Fox said it was not right to have ten moons of winter, that two were enough, and that people could then eat sunflower seeds, roots, and berries. Coyote repeated what he had said before, and they argued about it a long time. Finally Silver-Fox said: "You talk too much! I am going to make four moons for the whole year. I won't talk about it any more. There will be two moons of winter, and one of spring, and one of autumn. That's enough."

HOW KEMUSH CREATED THE WORLD

Klamath

IN the time that was, Kemush, Old Man of the Ancients, slept in Yamsi, Lodge of the North Wind. Hard had been his work. Kemush had made the world. He had sprung quickly from the ashes of the northern lights and made the world at the call of Morning Star. At first Kaila, the earth, had been flat and bare. Then Kemush planted in the valleys the grass, and camas roots, iba and ipo roots. On Molaiksi, Steepness, he had set Kapka, the pine, Wako, the white pine, and Ktalo, the juniper. On the rivers and lakes Kemush placed Weks, the mallard, and Waiwash, the white goose. Mushmush, the white-tail deer, Wan, the red fox, and Ketchkatch, the little gray fox, ran through the forest. Koil, the mountain sheep, and Luk, the grizzly bear, Kemush set on Kta-iti, place of rocks. So made Kemush the earth. And all the earth was new except Shapashkeni, the rock, where was built the lodge of Sun and Moon.

So Kemush slept while the day was young. Then came Wanaka, the sun halo, and called to the sleeping one, Old Man of the Ancients. Kemush rose from the door of the lodge. Together they followed the trail of Shel, the sun, until they reached the edge of the dark. But Maidu, the Indian, was not yet created.

Then Kemush, with his daughter, Evening Sky, went to the Place of the Dark, to the lodges of the Munatalkni. Five nights in a great circle about a vast fire they danced with the spirits of the dark. The spirits were without number, like the leaves on the trees. But when Shel called to the world, the spirits became dry bones.

On the fifth day, when the sun was new, Kemush rose and put the dry bones into a sack. Then as he followed the trail of Shel to the edge of the world, he threw away the bones. He threw them away two by two. To Kta-iti, place of steepness, he threw two. To Kuyani Shaiks, the crawfish trail, to Molaiksi, steepness of snow, and to Kakasam Yama, mountain of the great blue heron, to each he threw two bones. Thus people were created. The dry bones became Maidu, the Indian, Aikspala, the people of the chipmunks, and last of all, Maklaks, the Klamath Indian.

Then Kemush followed the trail of Shel, the sun, climbing higher and higher. At the top of the trail he built his lodge. Here still lives Kemush, Old Man of the Ancients, with his daughter Evening Sky, and Wanaka, the sun halo.

THE ROBE OF KEMUSH

Klamath

KEMUSH, walking upon the earth after having created it, saw five lynxes sitting upon a tree. Kemush had on only a rabbit blanket. Kemush tore his blanket to pieces, saying, "The lynxes will be a good robe to me when I kill them." Picking up a stone, he threw it at the lynxes. One lynx jumped down and ran away. Kemush said, "Oh! it will not be a good mantle." Again he missed with a stone. Another lynx, jumping down, ran off. Kemush said, "Again one skipped away. Now my mantle will become small." The three lynxes sitting on the tree scoffed at Kemush. Again with a stone he missed the lynxes. Another one jumped down and ran away. Kemush said, "It will only cover my back." Picking up another stone, he missed the lynxes. Both skipping down, ran away. Kemush began crying, "*Lo-i loyan loyak. Lo-loyan loyak.*" Again gathering the pieces of his blanket, he pinned it together with splinters. Then putting it around himself, started off.

Not far away an antelope with an aching tooth lay on a clearing. Spreading his rabbit blanket over the antelope, Kemush kicked it. Then he began searching for a stone knife with which to skin it. An antelope behind him ran off. Looking at it, Kemush said, "This looks like my antelope." Then the antelope of Kemush ran in front of him. Kemush saw his blanket on the antelope's back. He cried, "Stop! Stop! The people will make fun of you, wrapped in my old rabbit blanket."

HOW QAWANECA CREATED THE WORLD

AT first it was dark. There was neither wind nor rain. There were no people or animals. In the middle of the water, on a piece of land, sat Qawaneca. He sat by his fire breathing the smoke of burning cedar. On the edge of the land stood another god. Looking northward, he saw an ash tree. Looking southward, he saw a red cedar. Therefore the ash and red cedar are sacred above all other trees. Looking southwest, he saw something red. Said Qawaneca: "It must be land coming." At last the land came and touched the piece on which they sat. But it was unsteady. It trembled. Then Qawaneca pressed his hands over it, making it steady. He wanted to make more land but he did not wish sickness to be in it. He said: "Where many die, I will make much water and little land. Where few die, I will make much land and little water."

Qawaneca chose three rocks and two pieces of earth. He threw one rock into the water. Then

"Streams from the melting snow"

(*Page 33*)

North Buttress of the Bridge of the Gods

he listened. It went down, down, down! He threw another rock; then the third. Then he threw a piece of earth. He listened. He threw the other piece of earth. After the fifth throw, mighty waves arose. They dashed against the land, then receded. Thus were the tides formed.

Then more land came, but it was muddy. Man could not step on it. Soon footprints appeared. "Ha," said Qawaneca. "That is sickness. It is bad." So he made the water cover the land. Then he blew at the water and uncovered the land. Again footprints came in the mud. "That is bad. That is sickness," said Qawaneca. Four times he made water cover the land. The fifth time the footprints were made as before. Qawaneca let them alone. Five is a sacred number.

All this time it was dark. Qawaneca tried to make daylight, but could not. Then he called all the birds to a great council. He asked them how to make sunlight. Only one bird knew. He said in the far north was the sun. Two wild geese had been there. The geese said there was a magic way of calling the sun. They would teach Qawaneca if he would give special privileges to all birds. So Qawaneca learned the secret and called the sun. It came at his call and stopped as he told it. So

Qawaneca made a track for the sun, northward in summer, southward in winter.

Qawaneca pulled two hairs from his head and threw them on the ground. They became snakes. Soon there were many on the land and in the water. They made storms by blowing with their mouths. One long serpent coiled itself five times around the world, so it does not fall apart.

Qawaneca pulled two more hairs from his head. They became dogs.

Afterwards a woman came from the south. She is the Mother who never dies. She is the South. All Indians return to her at death and she sends them back as infants. Qawaneca now lives in the sun and looks down on the people.

HOW OLD MAN ABOVE CREATED THE WORLD

Shasta Indians

LONG, long ago, when the world was so new that even the stars were dark, it was very, very flat. Chareya, Old Man Above, could not see through the dark to the new, flat earth. Neither could he step down to it because it was so far below him. With a large stone he bored a hole in the sky. Then through the hole he pushed down masses of ice and snow, until a great pyramid rose from the plain. Old Man Above climbed down through the hole he had made in the sky, stepping from cloud to cloud, until he could put his foot on top the mass of ice and snow. Then with one long step he reached the earth.

The sun shone through the hole in the sky and began to melt the ice and snow. It made holes in the ice and snow. When it was soft, Chareya bored with his finger into the earth, here and there, and planted the first trees. Streams from the melting snow watered the new trees and made them grow.

Then he gathered the leaves which fell from the trees and blew upon them. They became birds. He took a stick and broke it into pieces. Out of the small end he made fishes and placed them in the mountain streams. Of the middle of the stick, he made all the animals except the grizzly bear. From the big end of the stick came the grizzly bear, who was made master of all. Grizzly was large and strong and cunning. When the earth was new he walked upon two feet and carried a large club. So strong was Grizzly that Old Man Above feared the creature he had made. Therefore, so that he might be safe, Chareya hollowed out the pyramid of ice and snow as a tepee. There he lived for thousands of snows. The Indians knew he lived there because they could see the smoke curling from the smoke hole of his tepee. When the pale-face came, Old Man Above went away. There is no longer any smoke from the smoke hole. White men call the tepee Mount Shasta.

OLD MAN ABOVE AND THE GRIZZLIES

Shasta Indians

A LONG time ago, while smoke still curled from the smoke hole of the tepee, a great storm arose. The storm shook the tepee. Wind blew the smoke down the smoke hole. Old Man Above said to Little Daughter: "Climb up to the smoke hole. Tell Wind to be quiet. Stick your arm out of the smoke hole before you tell him." Little Daughter climbed up to the smoke hole and put out her arm. But Little Daughter put out her head also. She wanted to see the world. Little Daughter wanted to see the rivers and trees, and the white foam on the Bitter Waters. Wind caught Little Daughter by the hair. Wind pulled her out of the smoke hole and blew her down the mountain. Wind blew Little Daughter over the smooth ice and the great forests, down to the land of the Grizzlies. Wind tangled her hair and then left her cold and shivering near the tepees of the Grizzlies.

Soon Grizzly came home. In those days Grizzly walked on two feet, and carried a big stick. Grizzly could talk as people do. Grizzly laid down the young elk he had killed and picked up Little Daughter. He took Little Daughter to his tepee. Then Mother Grizzly warmed her by the fire. Mother Grizzly gave her food to eat.

Soon Little Daughter married the son of Grizzly. Their children were not Grizzlies. They were men. So the Grizzlies built a tepee for Little Daughter and her children. White men call the tepee Little Shasta.

At last Mother Grizzly sent a son to Old Man Above. Mother Grizzly knew that Little Daughter was the child of Old Man Above, but she was afraid. She said: "Tell Old Man Above that Little Daughter is alive."

Old Man Above climbed out of the smoke hole. He ran down the mountain side to the land of the Grizzlies. Old Man Above ran very quickly. Wherever he set his foot the snow melted. The snow melted very quickly and made streams of water. Now Grizzlies stood in line to welcome Old Man Above. They stood on two feet and carried clubs. Then Old Man Above saw his daughter and her children. He saw the new race of men. Then Old Man Above became very angry. He said to Grizzlies:

"Never speak again. Be silent. Neither shall ye stand upright. Ye shall use your hands as feet. Ye shall look downward."

Then Old Man Above put out the fire in the tepee. Smoke no longer curls from the smoke hole. He fastened the door of the tepee. The new race of men he drove out. Then Old Man Above took Little Daughter back to his tepee.

That is why grizzlies walk on four feet and look downward. Only when fighting they stand on two feet and use their fists like men.

DURATION OF LIFE

Klamath

KEMUSH, Old Man of the Ancients, ruled as follows: The Klamath Lake people, Maklaks, from a service-berry bush, from Tschak, he made. He made the Kakalish people from skunks. Northward while he had gone, he created them on his way. Klamath Lake people he laid down in the sun heat. The white people he laid in the shade. Therefore the Maklaks are dark. The white race is light and beyond the sea he made a world for them.

Kemush made mole also, flybug also, garter snake also. When he had made them, they began to argue about man.

Mole said: "I want human beings to live to great age."

Garter Snake thus spoke: "I order man to be thus made." Garter Snake began shedding its skin, saying: "This way I want man to become, after having grown to be of great age — always to grow young again."

On that subject Mole said: "And I want human beings to be thus made — decrepit by age." Shivering, he said, "Thus I want human beings to shiver."

Flybug also voted with Mole. Flybug said: "Many human beings, acting cruelly, will step on me and crush me." Thus they argued.

HOW COYOTE STOLE FIRE

LONG ago men were hungry and unhappy. They were cold. The only fire in the world was on a mountain top, watched by three Skookums. They guarded the fire carefully. Men might steal it and become as strong as they.

Coyote wanted men to be warm and happy. One day he crept to the mountain top and watched the Skookums. He watched all day and all night. They thought he was only a skulking coyote. Coyote saw that one Skookum sat always by the fire. When one went into the tepee, another came out and sat by the fire. Only when the dawn wind arose was there a chance to steal fire. Then Skookum, shivering, hurried into the tepee. She called: "Sister, sister, get up and watch the fire." But the sister was slow.

Coyote went down the mountain side and called a great council of the animals. He knew if he stole fire, the Skookums would chase him. Coyote said the other animals must help him.

Again Coyote skulked to the mountain top. The Skookums saw only a coyote shivering in the bushes.

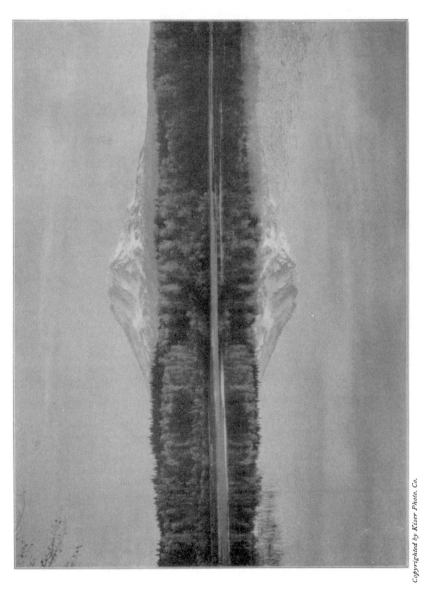

MOUNT ADAMS

KULSHAN "THE GREAT WHITE WATCHER." (MOUNT BAKER)

When the dawn wind rose, the Skookum on guard called: " Sister, sister, get up and watch the fire." But the sister was slow. Then Coyote seized the fire and jumped down the mountain side. Quickly Skookum followed him. She caught the tip of his tail in her hand; therefore it is white, even to this day. But Coyote reached Wolf. Wolf seized the fire and leaped down the mountain. Skookum chased Wolf. But Wolf reached Squirrel. Squirrel seized the fire and leaped from branch to branch down the mountain. The fire was so hot it burned the back of his neck. You can see the black spot there, even to this day. The fire was so hot it made Squirrel's tail curl up over his back. Skookum chased Squirrel. But Squirrel reached Frog. Frog took the coals of fire in his mouth and hopped away. Skookum chased Frog. She caught his tail in her hand. Frog jumped away but Skookum kept the tail. That is why frogs have no tail, even to this day. Soon Skookum caught up with Frog again. To save the fire, Frog spit it out on Wood. Wood swallowed it. Skookum did not know how to get the fire out of Wood. But Coyote did. Coyote showed the Indians how to get fire out of Wood by rubbing two dry sticks together, as they do even to this day.

HOW BEAVER STOLE FIRE

Nez Percés

LONG ago there were no people in the world. Animals and trees talked just as men do now. They also walked about. Now in those days, Pine Trees had the secret of fire. They would tell no one else. No one could have a fire, no matter how cold it was, unless he were a Pine. One winter it was so cold the animals almost froze to death. Then they called a council. They wanted to steal fire from Pine Trees.

Now on Grande Ronde River, Pine Trees were holding also a great council. They had built a large fire to warm themselves. Guards were put around the fire to keep off all animals. But Beaver hid under the bank, near the fire, before the guards took their places, so they did not see him. After a while a live coal rolled down the bank near Beaver. He hid it in his breast and ran away. Pine Trees started after him. When Pine Trees caught up near him, Beaver dodged from side to side. Other times he ran straight ahead. That is why Grande Ronde River winds from side to side in some places. In other places it is straight.

When they had run a long way, Pine Trees grew tired. They stopped on the river banks. So many stopped there, and so close together, that even to-day hunters can hardly get through the trees. A few kept on after Beaver and stopped here and there. These also remain here and there on the river bank.

A few Pine Trees kept close after Beaver. So did Cedar. Cedar said, "I will run to the top of that hill. I will see how far ahead he is." So Cedar ran to the top of the hill. Beaver was far ahead. He was just diving into Big Snake River where Grande Ronde joins it. Beaver swam across Big Snake River and gave fire to Willows on the opposite bank. Farther on he gave fire to Birches and to other trees. So these woods have fire in them. Ever since then animals and Indians can get fire from these woods by rubbing two pieces together.

Cedar still stands all alone on the very top of the hill. He is very old. His top is dead. The chase was a long one. You can see that because there are no other cedars within a hundred miles of him. Old men of the tribes point him out to the children. They say, "There is Old Cedar. He stands just where he stopped when he chased Beaver."

HOW DOG STOLE FIRE

Pit River
(Achomawi)

PINE–MARTEN stole the two wives of Hawk-Man. Hawk-Man grew very angry, and at once put on his shaman's ornaments and began to dance and to sing, "*Ketj ketja winino, ketj ketja winino.*"

At once it began to rain. Only Weasel noticed it and spoke of it. All night it poured. The water rose higher and higher until it ran in at the door. "Tell them to go back, these two women! That Hawk-Man will kill us, he will drown us."

But Pine-Marten said nothing until morning. Then he said, "I do not like this. Where is a brave man? I want him to go and kill Hawk-Man."

So a man got up and went over, taking a knife and a shield. Hawk-Man was dancing harder and harder, and at every leap his head came up through the smoke hole. The man crept nearer and nearer, and finally struck Hawk-Man. He cut off his head.

44

"THE SUN MADE HOLES IN THE ICE AND SNOW"

(*Page 33*)

"THE ONLY FIRE IN THE WORLD WAS ON A MOUNTAIN TOP"

(Page 40)

At once the rain stopped and the clouds cleared away, and the water sank. Then people said, "If a shaman is bad, we will kill him. That is how it shall be." Then they went off to hunt.

After Hawk-Man had been killed and the waters had sunk again, people found that the fires were put out all over the world. Nothing could be cooked. For a time they did not trouble about it, but in a few days they began to talk about it. They sent Owl to Shasta to look out all over the world and see if he could find any trace of fire. Owl took a feather blanket and went. Lizard watched him go and told the people how he was getting on. After a long while, when Owl did not come back, people thought he was dead. But Lizard said, "Sh! I can see him." Owl got to the top at last, very tired and wet with sweat. He looked all around. Twice he looked to the west and there saw smoke coming from a sweat house. After a while Owl came down from the mountain and told the people what he had seen.

Next morning all got ready and went off to the west, to where the smoke had been seen. Every one had a cedar-bark torch. Dog had some punk hidden in his ear. Late in the evening they arrived at the lodge and asked to be allowed to warm their hands. Dog held his ear down and fire caught in the punk.

Then every one thrust their torches into the fire and ran. The people in the lodge were angry and struck at them as they ran off. Coyote's fire gave out first, then the fire of one after another gave out until all the torches were out. The people who owned the fire had made it rain and this put out the torches. No one knew that Dog had fire. They got home and were much troubled, for they thought the fire had all been lost. Dog was laughing and said, " I am sweating." Coyote got angry at this and said, " Hit him! Put him out!"

Then Dog said to Fox, " Look in my ear." When he did so, he saw the fire. He took out the punk, made fire from it, and so people got fire again.

THE BRIDGE OF THE GODS

LONG ago, when the world was new, Tyhee Sahale with his two sons, came down Great River. They came near where the Dalles now are. The land was very beautiful and each son wanted it. Therefore they quarrelled. Then Sahale took his bow and shot two arrows. One he shot to the north; the other he shot to the west. Then Sahale said to his sons, "Go. Find the arrows. Where they lie, you shall have the land."

One son went north over the plain to the country of the Klickitats. He was the first grandfather of the Klickitats. The other son followed the arrow to the Willamette Valley. He was the first grandfather of the Multnomahs.

Then Sahale raised great mountains between the country of the Klickitats and the country of the Multnomahs. This he did that the tribes might not quarrel. White men call them the Cascade Mountains. But Great River was deep and broad. The river was a sign of peace between the tribes. Therefore Sahale made a great stone bridge over the river, that the tribes might be friends. This was called the Bridge of the Tomanowos.

The tribes grew, but they did evil things. They displeased Tyhee Sahale. Therefore the sun ceased to shine, and cold and snow appeared. The people were unhappy for they had no fire. Only Loo-wit had fire. Therefore the people sought to steal the fire of Loo-wit. Then Loo-wit fled and because the runners were stiff with cold, they could not catch her.

Then Loo-wit told Sahale of the need of the Indians. Loo-wit said the Indians were cold. So Sahale gave fire to the people. Thus Sahale built a fire on the bridge of the gods, and there the people secured fire. Sahale also promised to Loo-wit eternal youth and beauty. Thus Loo-wit became a beautiful maiden.

Then began the chiefs to love Loo-wit. Many chiefs loved her because she was so beautiful. Then came two more chiefs, Klickitat from the north and Wiyeast from the west. To neither would Loo-wit give an answer. Therefore the chiefs fought, and their people also fought. Thus did they anger Sahale. Therefore, because blood was shed and because Great River was no longer a sign of peace, Sahale broke down the tomanowos illahee. Great rocks fell into the river. They are there even to this day.

When the water is quiet, buried forests can be seen even to this day. Thus Sahale destroyed the bridge of the gods. Thus the tribes were separated by Great River.

Then Sahale made of Loo-wit, Klickitat, and Wiyeast snow peaks. Always they were to be cold and covered with ice and snow. White men call them Mount St. Helens, Mount Adams, and Mount Hood.

THE DALLES

LONG ago, after Sahale had broken down the bridge of the gods, Klickitat and Wiyeast still quarrelled over Loo-wit. When they quarrelled, sheets of flame burst from their peaks, and they threw great rocks at one another. But Klickitat and Wiyeast did not throw far enough. The rocks fell into the Great River, and blocked it. Therefore the river is very narrow and very swift at that point. Thus it is called the Dalles.

THE STORY OF ASHISH

Klamath

ASHISH, they say, having many people with him, gambled. While on their way gambling, they built fires. Purple-blue was the fire of Ashish; the fire of Silver-Fox was yellow only; the fire of Kemush was smoke only.

Then they shot at the target. Ashish hit it straight; Silver-Fox slightly missed the mark; Kemush hit this side of the mark. All the others struck far this side of the mark. After doing so they began gambling again. They bet on many things. Then Ashish won over them. About noon all the men had lost all they had. Then they went to their lodges.

Now Ashish had five wives. Mud Hen was one wife of Ashish; Long-tail Squirrel was one wife; Sandhill Crane was one wife; Mallard was one wife; Chaffinch was one wife.

Then Kemush plotted secretly. After daybreak he plotted against Ashish. Then Kemush began to weep, pretending to remember the inherited place

where his father had killed eagles. Now declared
Kemush to Ashish, "Far away is the killing place of
the young eagles. I kill them not, being afraid."
Then they set out together, Kemush and Ashish.
Now Kemush coveted Little Squirrel, the wife of
Ashish.

Then they saw eagles. Kemush pointed out the
pine for Ashish to climb up. Then the eagles
flew on the pine. Ashish climbed up, but as he
climbed the tree grew. Far up, the pine now
touched the sky. Ashish having climbed to the top,
saw only the young ones of a lark, although it was
the eyrie of an eagle. Thus Ashish wept, sitting in
the eyrie.

Then Kemush went away. He dressed himself
to appear like Ashish. He came back to the lodge
from the pine tree.

Now the wives of Ashish became suspicious.
"This one is Kemush,"—thus said the wives of
Ashish. Next morning they all went with those
who were in the habit of gambling with Ashish.
They built a fire while gambling. And from the
fire of Kemush smoke only curled up. Then they
suspected, and said, "This is not Ashish. This is
Kemush," — thus said those afar off, "Ashish did
not come. The fire of Ashish is not burning there."

TIN-TIN-MIT-SI, CAYUSE WARRIOR

The fox tail was formerly very significant, indicating a warrior's bravery

YAKIMA WARRIOR WITH CEREMONIAL PIPE AND BEADED
TOBACCO POUCH

Thus said the followers in the distance. Those in the distance also said, " Ye will find out this man after he has shot at the mark. Ashish always hits straight."

Then they shot. Kemush struck far this side of the mark. Silver-Fox missed a little. Then they commenced gambling and they won over Kemush. All day long they won many stakes. Then they went back to the lodges. Then they quit gambling for they missed Ashish.

Now Ashish's wives wept constantly and left their lodges to dig roots. Four wives put pitch on their heads. Only Mallard mourned not for Ashish.

Then Ashish heard the weeping cries of Sandhill Crane, and Ashish wept hearing them. Now Ashish was far away close to the sky. He was nothing but bones. Then two butterflies flew up close to the sky and saw Ashish. Then they flew back, having seen him. They returned home and said to their father, " A good man will soon perish. Far off, close to the sky, we saw that man, nothing but bones. He will soon die." Thus they said to their father.

The father ordered them early next morning to fly up with a basket strung around them. So the butterflies carried up there food, carrying water also. They raised up Ashish in that eyrie. Then inquired those butterflies, "What are you doing up here?"

Then Ashish said, "Kemush sent me after the eagles. And I climbed the small pine and it grew up under me. The pine grew up during my climbing. Then I saw eagles. Of the lark saw I only the young." So Ashish said, giving explanations to them.

Then the butterflies spread a wildcat's skin in the willow basket. They placed Ashish in it, after giving him food, giving him water also. Then they took him in the basket down to the ground. Thus he returned. Then he lay sick a long time, then he recovered.

CREATION OF MANKIND

Pit River
(*Achomawi*)

SILVER-FOX and Coyote lived together. Silver-Fox gathered some service-berry sticks and whittled them down, working all night. The shavings were to be made into common people. The finished sticks were to be warriors and chiefs. About sunset the next day he was ready to make them alive. They turned into people. Then Silver-Fox sent them away, some in one direction and some in another. Then he and Coyote had a big feast.

But Coyote wanted also to make people, so he did everything he had seen Silver-Fox do. He gathered some service-berry sticks and whittled them down, working all night. About sunset the next day he was ready to make them alive. They turned into people. Then Coyote ran after some of the women and after a long chase caught them. But so soon as he touched them, they turned into shavings.

AS-AI-YAHAL

Tillamook

AS-AI-YAHAL, the god, lived far up in the country. A long time ago he travelled all over the world. He came down the river and arrived at Natahts. There he gathered clams and mussels. He made a fire and roasted them. When he opened them, he found two animals in each shell. After he had roasted them he began to eat and soon had enough. That made him angry and he said, "Henceforth there shall be only one animal in each shell."

The god came to Tillamook Bay and then went up the river. He had to cross it far up because he had no canoe and the river was deep. He met a number of women who were digging roots.

He asked, "What are you doing there?"

They replied, "We are digging roots."

He said, "I do not like that." He took the roots away and sent them to Clatsop. Ever since that time there have been no roots at Tillamook while at Clatsop they are very plentiful.

56

MOUNT SHASTA AND LITTLE SHASTA

"IT WAS SO COLD THE ANIMALS ALMOST FROZE TO DEATH"

(*Page 42*)

He went on and came to a river full of salmon which were clapping their fins. He caught one of them, threw it ashore, stepped on it, and flattened it. It became a flounder. Ever since then flounders have been plentiful at Tillamook while there have been no salmon there.

As-ai-yahal travelled on and came to a house in which he saw people lying around the fire.

He asked, "What is the matter? Are you sick?"

"No," they replied, "we are starving. East Wind wants to kill us. The river, sea, and beach are frozen over and we cannot get any food."

Then he said, "Can't you make East Wind stop blowing so you can secure food?"

He went out of the house and far up the river, which was frozen over. It was so slippery he could hardly stand. He went up the river to meet East Wind and to conquer him. Before he came to the house of East Wind, he took up some pieces of ice which he threw into the river, saying, "Henceforth it shall not be as cold as it is now. Winter shall be a little cold but not very much so. You shall become herring." The ice at once became herring and swam down the river.

As-ai-yahal went on until he reached the house of East Wind. He entered and whistled. He was trembling with cold, but did not go near the fire. He said, "I am so warm I cannot go near the fire." Then he told East Wind he came from a house where they were drying herring.

East Wind said, "Don't say so. It is winter now. There will be no herring for a long time to come."

As-ai-yahal replied, "Don't you believe me? There are plenty of herring outside." He took an icicle which he warmed at the fire. "Look how quickly it boils," he said to East Wind as the ice melted. He made East Wind believe that the melting ice was a herring.

Then East Wind ceased to blow, the ice began to melt, and the people had plenty of food. Until then, it had been winter all the year; now we have both summer and winter.

THE GOLDEN AGE

Tinne

LONG ago the world was only a great sheet of water. There was no land. There were no people. Only the Thunder Bird lived. The beating of its wings was thunder. Its glance was lightning. Then the Thunder Bird flew down and touched the water. Thus the earth arose. Then the Thunder Bird flew down again and touched the earth. Thus the animals were created. Thus Thunder Bird created all living things except people. Dog was the ancestor of the Tinne.

Then Thunder Bird gave to the Tinne a sacred arrow. This arrow was never to be used or lost. Thus the Tinne, because of the sacred arrow, never died. Men wore out their throats with eating. Men lived so long their feet wore out from walking. Thus the Tinne were happy. Then they disobeyed Thunder Bird. They used the sacred arrow, therefore Arrow flew away. Thus the Tinne now die as do other Indians.

THE FIRST TOTEM POLE*

Kwakiutl

ONCE there was a chief who had never had a dance. All the other chiefs had big dances, but Wakiash none. Therefore Wakiash was unhappy. He thought for a long while about the dance. Then he went up into the mountains to fast. Four days he fasted. On the fourth day he fell asleep. Then something fell on his breast. It was a green frog. Frog said, "Wake up." Then Wakiash waked up. He looked about to see where he was. Frog said, "You are on Raven's back. Raven will fly around the world with you."

So Raven flew. Raven flew all around the world. Raven showed Wakiash everything in the world. On the fourth day, Raven flew past a house with a totem pole in front of it. Wakiash could hear singing in the house. Wakiash wished he could take the totem pole and the house with him. Now Frog knew what Wakiash was thinking. Frog told Raven. Raven stopped and Frog told Wakiash to hide behind the

* As told by Natalie Curtis.

TOTEM POLES

THE BASKET MAKER

door. Frog said, "When they dance, jump out into the room."

The people in the house began to dance. They were animal people. But they could not sing or dance. One said, "Something is the matter. Some one is near us."

Chief said, "Let one who can run faster than the flames go around the house and see."

So Mouse went. Mouse could go anywhere, even into a box. Now Mouse looked like a woman; she had taken off her animal clothes. Mouse ran out, but Wakiash caught her.

Wakiash said, "Wait. I will give you something." So he gave her a piece of mountain goat's fat. Wakiash said to Mouse, "I want the totem pole and the house. I want the dances and the songs."

Mouse said, "Wait until I come again."

Mouse went back into the house. She said, "I could find nobody." So the animal people tried again to dance. They tried three times. Each time, Chief sent Mouse out to see if some one was near. Each time, Mouse talked with Wakiash. The third time Mouse said, "When they begin to dance, jump into the room."

So the animal people began to dance. Then Wakiash sprang into the room. The dancers were ashamed. They had taken off their animal clothes and looked like men. So the animal people were silent. Then Mouse said, "What does this man want?" Now Wakiash wanted the totem pole and the house. He wanted the dances and the songs. Mouse knew what Wakiash was thinking. Mouse told the animal people.

Chief said, "Let the man sit down. We will show him how to dance." So they danced. Then Chief asked Wakiash what kind of a dance he would like to choose. They were using masks for the dance. Wakiash wanted the Echo mask, and the Little Man mask, — the little man who talks, talks, and quarrels with others. Mouse told the people what Wakiash was thinking.

Then Chief said, "You can take the totem pole and the house also. You can take the masks and dances, for one dance." Then Chief folded up the house very small. He put it in a dancer's headdress. Chief said, "When you reach home, throw down this bundle. The house will unfold and you can give a dance."

Then Wakiash went back to Raven. Wakiash climbed on Raven's back and went to sleep. When he awoke, Raven and Frog were gone. Wakiash was alone. It was night and the tribe was asleep. Then Wakiash threw down the bundle. Behold! the house and totem pole were there. The whale painted on the house was blowing. The animals on the totem pole were making noises. At once the tribe woke up. They came to see Wakiash. Wakiash found he had been gone four years instead of four days.

Then Wakiash gave a great dance. He taught the people the songs. Echo came to the dance. He repeated all the sounds they made. When they finished the dance, behold! the house was gone. It went back to the animal people. Thus all the chiefs were ashamed because Wakiash had the best dance.

Then Wakiash made out of wood a house and another totem pole. They called it Kalakuyuwish, "the pole that holds up the sky."

SPIRIT OF SNOW

SPIRIT of Snow did not like people. He was very stingy. Spirit of Snow did not wish that people should eat of the deer and elk. Therefore the Indians did not like him. Therefore when too much snow fell, Indians outwitted Spirit of Snow. They said a charm to him. They said this to Spirit of Snow, " Hither drive the elk, the Black-Necked ones that dwell back to the mountains, in dark places under the trees."

Thus it was customary to speak to Snow. Then it no longer snowed. Again he became quiet. Snow is stingy. He does not desire to drive down elk.

OWL AND RAVEN

Eskimo

OWL and Raven were close friends. One day Raven made a new dress, dappled black and white, for Owl. Owl, in return, made for Raven a pair of whalebone boots and then began to make for her a white dress. When Owl wanted to fit the dress, Raven hopped about and would not sit still. Owl became very angry and said, "If I fly over you with a blubber lamp, don't jump." Raven continued to hop about. At last Owl became very angry and emptied the blubber lamp over the new white dress. Raven cried, "Qaq! Qaq!" Ever since that day Raven has been black all over.

CRADLE SONG

Modoc

EARLY in the morning robin will eat ants,
Early, early will it pick at the cedar tree,
Early in the morning it chatters, " Tchiwip, tchiwip,
    Tchitch, tsits, techitch."

Pho'o by Lee Moorhouse

UMATILLA SQUAW AND PAPPOOSE

Yakima Maiden

"Many chiefs loved Loo-wit because she was so beautiful"

(Page 48)

WOODRAT AND RABBITS

Modoc

A WOODRAT lived with its mother. Five cotton-tail rabbits lived near by. Rat said to Rabbit, " Let us have a quarrel."

Rabbit said, " Why do you want to quarrel with me?"

Woodrat replied, " That's all right. Let us have a fuss. Don't you always prefer the bitter leaves of some sort of cabbage to everything else?"

Rabbit answered, " You must be a thief. Only yesterday I saw you watching carefully for the right moment to steal something. Your big ears were bent sidewise."

Woodrat replied, " And you I see always skipping about with your crooked legs to snatch leaves from the cabbage bush."

Rabbit said, " You are an old fool. You are good for nothing except to eat holes in your grandmother's dress. That is why you want to attack me."

Woodrat went to a distance and spread out a net to

catch Rabbit. Then he seized a stick, drove Rabbit into the net, and beat him to death.

Woodrat went to the Second Rabbit. "Let us have a fight."

"Why should we fight?" asked Second Rabbit.

They fought because Second Rabbit said Woodrat ate up his grandmother's long dress.

Woodrat went to Third Rabbit. "You are nothing but a fool — a good-for-nothing eater of cabbage leaves," said Woodrat.

Rabbit answered, "You are a thief. You live in an old wooden shed."

So Woodrat started a quarrel with all the cotton-tail rabbits. Thus Woodrat killed all five cotton-tail rabbits.

Then Woodrat and his mother ate them up. They danced over them a medicine dance. While they danced, Woodrat's wooden lodge caught fire. Thus Woodrat and his mother were burned to death.

This is the end of the tale.

QUARREL OF SUN AND MOON

Siouan

IN the days of the first grandfather, Niaba, the Moon, and Mi, the Sun, lived upon the earth. Then they quarrelled.

Said Niaba: "I am out of patience with you. I gather the people but you scatter them. You cause them to be lost."

Said Mi, the Sun: "I wish for many people to grow, so I scatter them. You put them in darkness; thus you kill many with hunger." Then Mi called to the people, "Ho! Ye who are people. Many of you shall grow strong. I will look down on you from above. I will rule all your work."

Said Niaba: "And I, too, will dwell above you. I will gather you when it is dark. Assembling in full numbers, you shall sleep. I myself will rule all your work. We will walk in the trail, one after the other. I will walk behind him."

So Niaba follows Mi on the trail in the sky. Niaba is just like a woman. She always walks with a kettle on her arm.

CHINOOK WIND

Yakima

ONCE five brothers lived on Great River. They were the Chinook brothers and they caused the warm wind to blow. There were five other brothers who lived on Great River. They lived at Walla Walla, the meeting of the waters. They caused the cold wind to blow. Now the grandparents of all these brothers lived at Umatilla, the place of wind-drifted sands.

Walla Walla brothers and Chinook brothers were always fighting. They made the winds to sweep over the country, they blew down trees and raised great clouds of dust, they froze the rivers and thawed them so as to make floods. It was very hard for the people.

At last Walla Walla brothers said to Chinook brothers: "We will wrestle with you. Whoever falls down shall have his head cut off. Thus he shall be dead." So Coyote was made judge. He was also to cut the heads off those who fell down.

Now Coyote secretly told the grandparents of

"Young Chinook could pull up large fir trees and throw them around like weeds"

(*Page 71*)

AN INDIAN MADONNA

Yakima

Chinook brothers to throw oil on the ground. Then their sons would not fall. Coyote also secretly told the grandparents of Walla Walla brothers to throw ice on the ground. Then their sons would not fall. The oil and the ice made the ground very slippery. But the Walla Walla grandparents had thrown ice on the ground last. So Chinook brothers fell down. First one fell and then another, until all fell down. Then Coyote cut off their heads.

Now the oldest Chinook brother had a baby son. The baby's mother taught him he must revenge his father and uncles. So Young Chinook grew very strong. At last he felt himself very strong. He could pull up large fir trees and throw them around like weeds.

Then Young Chinook went up Great River. Wherever he went he pulled up large fir trees and threw them around like weeds. In the valley of the Yakima he turned aside and went to sleep by Setas, the creek. The mark of his sleeping-place can still be seen on the mountain side.

Then Young Chinook came back to the Great River and went to Umatilla, the place of wind-drifted sands. Here he found his grandparents very cold and hungry. Walla Walla brothers caused the northeast wind to blow all the time. They also stole their fish, when they were returning to the shore. Always they stole the fish.

Young Chinook said: "We will go fishing now." So grandfather started out to fish. Young Chinook lay down in the bottom of the boat. When the boat was full of fish, grandfather started back for the shore. Then Walla Walla brothers started out from the shore to rob grandfather. But they could not catch the boat. Every time Walla Walla brothers came near the boat, it would shoot ahead. So grandfather reached the shore with his fish. Then Young Chinook took his grandparents to the river and bathed them. All the straw and grass and bark which he washed off became trout. That is how trout came to be in Great River.

Now Walla Walla brothers knew that Young Chinook was alive. They sent a messenger to him. They said: "We will wrestle with you. Whoever falls down shall have his head cut off. Thus he shall be dead." So Coyote was made judge. He was also to cut off the heads of those who fell down.

Now Coyote secretly told the grandparents of Walla Walla brothers to throw ice on the ground. Coyote also secretly told the grandparents of Young Chinook to throw oil on the ground. But he told them to throw oil last. So young Chinook wrestled with Walla Walla brothers, one after another. So the Walla Walla brothers fell to the ground. First one fell and then another, until four had fallen. Then Coyote cut off their heads. The fifth one yielded without wrestling. So Coyote let him live. But Coyote said: "You must blow only lightly. You must never freeze people again."

To Young Chinook, Coyote said: "You shall blow hardest only at night. You shall blow first on the mountain ridges to warn the people."

Thus now winter is only a little cold.

THE MISER OF TAKHOMA

Cowlitz

LONG, long ago, Miser lived near the foot of Takhoma. He never was happy. When food was scarce and the tribe were starving, Miser could find fish in secret places in the streams. When the snows were deep and the black-necked elk hid in the dark places of the forest, he could still secure meat. His skill as a hunter and fisherman was known to all his tribe. But Miser cared only for hiaqua. Now Moosmoos, the elk, was Miser's tomanowos. Therefore he tried to talk with the elk, even while hunting them. He wanted more hiaqua.

One night Moosmoos whispered to Miser the secret hiding-place of the hiaqua of the tomanowos. The hiding-place was high up on Takhoma. Early in the morning, Miser began to make ready for his search. He sent his klootchman to dig camas roots. Thus he could work secretly. He made two elk-horn picks by taking off all the prongs except the upper ones. He filled his ikta with kinnikinnick,

74

and with dried salmon. At sunset Miser began to climb the mountain.

All night he climbed the trail. All the next day he climbed. By night again he was above the snow line, cold and tired and hungry. When the moon arose, he climbed again. Over vast snow fields, across wide cracks in the ice, over the slippery shoulders of the lower peaks he climbed. At sunrise he reached the top. Now Takhoma was the home of the tomanowos, therefore Miser was afraid. But Moosmoos had told him where the hiaqua was hidden.

In the white snow field which covered the crater was a black lake. Beyond it were three stones of equal height, all as tall as a giant. The top of the first was shaped like a salmon's head. The top of the second was like a camas root, and the third, like an elk's head. Then Miser believed the voice of Moosmoos.

Miser threw down his ikta. He unwrapped his elk-horn pick. Then he began to dig in the snow at the foot of the elk's head.

Miser struck the first blow. As an echo he heard a sudden puff. Startled, he turned to see a huge otter climbing out of the black waters of the lake. Big Otter struck his tail with a loud thump on the snow. Another otter appeared, then another. At last twelve otters gathered in a circle around their huge leader. They formed a circle around Miser, digging with his pick at the foot of the elk's head. Then Big Otter leaped to the top of the elk's head. All the otters gave a loud puff.

Miser kept digging. At every thirteenth blow of the pick Big Otter thumped with his tail on the elk's head. Then the circle of twelve thumped with theirs on the snow.

Miser became tired and stopped digging for a moment. Big Otter turned on the elk's head. With his tail he struck Miser on the shoulder. Then the twelve turned, walked backward, and struck him with their tails. Miser began to dig again.

As he dug in the rock, his pick broke. Big Otter jumped from the elk's head. He seized the second pick in his mouth and gave it to him.

Miser dared not stop. With each thirteenth blow of the pick and the thump of the tails, the otters came nearer. He could feel their breath as he lifted the last stone. Beneath lay a great hole, filled with hiaqua. As he lifted out the shells, the otters returned to their larger circle.

Miser lifted out handful after handful of the shell money. He strung the hiaqua on elk sinews, twenty strings in all. The rest he covered again. He

Copyright by Romans Photographic Co.

TAKHOMA

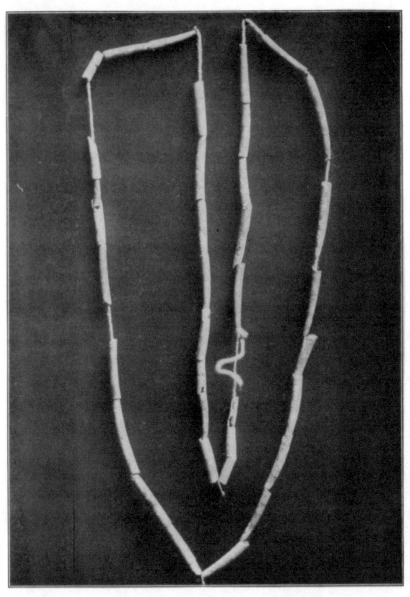

HIAQUA SHELLS

Taken from an old Indian grave at Fort Columbia

hurried, for it was after noon and he must return below the snow line. Then Miser left the elk's head. He offered no shells to Moosmoos or to Sahale. He had forgotten the tomanowos.

As he crossed the crater, the otters, one by one, with a loud puff, jumped into the black lake. They began to beat the black water with their tails. He heard them beat the water as he plunged through the snow to the edge of the crater. Miser felt that the shells were very heavy.

As he stepped over the edge of the crater, he glanced back. The three stones had vanished. A thick mist rose from the black waters of the lake. Under the mist was a black cloud, hiding the water. Miser feared tomanowos in the clouds.

Then the storm seized him. It flung him over an ice bank. The blackness of all darkness lay around him. Colenass, the storm god, came down upon the mountain. Tootah, the thunder, deafened him with its roar. The storm crashed about him. Fiery blasts melted the snow into great torrents. Icy winds froze them solid again. In the roar and thunder, Miser heard the voice of Kakahete, hyas tomanowos. Heard also the voices of all the tomanowos, "Ha, ha, hiaqua! Ha, ha, hiaqua!"

Miser threw away a string of hiaqua. The storm

slackened for a moment. Then all began again, louder than ever. Kakahete screamed, "Ha, ha, hiaqua! Ha, ha, hiaqua!"

One by one, Miser threw away the strings of hiaqua, strung on the sinews of Moosmoos, the elk. Always the tomanowos screamed after him. Then when the last string was gone, with a last gust the storm blew him down, flat upon the ground.

Miser slept a long time. When he awoke, Takhoma glistened above him, shining white in the sunlight. All around him grew camas roots. Rocky ridges lay where once the forest had stretched. Sunny meadows lay around him. Miser stretched himself and arose. Only dry leaves and dead grass remained in the rotted ikta. Miser wondered. Then he went down the mountain side. He ate berries for food until he came to a cabin in the valley. There lived a very old woman. He talked with her and found she was his klootchman. Klootchman said he had slept thirty snows. Miser looked at himself in a pool. He was very old. His hair was white. Many, many snows had the angry tomanowos made him sleep. But Miser was happy. He no longer cared for hiaqua.

WHY THERE ARE NO SNAKES ON TAK-HOMA

ALONG, long time ago, Tyhee Sahale became angry with the people. Sahale ordered a medicine man to take his bow and arrow and shoot into the cloud which hung low over Takhoma. The medicine man shot the arrow, and it stuck fast in the cloud. Then he shot another into the lower end of the first. Then he shot another into the lower end of the second. He shot arrows until he had made a chain which reached from the cloud to the earth. The medicine man told his klootchman and his children to climb up the arrow trail. Then he told the good animals to climb up the arrow trail. Then the medicine man climbed up himself. Just as he was climbing into the cloud, he looked back. A long line of bad animals and snakes were also climbing up the arrow trail. Therefore the medicine man broke the chain of arrows. Thus the snakes and bad animals fell down on the mountain side. Then at once it began to rain. It rained until all the land was flooded. Water reached even to the snow line of Takhoma. When all the bad animals and snakes were drowned, it stopped raining. After a while the waters sank again. Then the medicine man, and his klootchman, and the children climbed out of the cloud and came down the mountain side. The good animals also climbed out of the cloud. Thus there are now no snakes or bad animals on Takhoma.

CRY-BECAUSE-HE-HAD-NO-WIFE

Nez Percé

ONCE there was a little boy. He was an orphan. This boy cried day and night and would never be quiet. His grandmother asked him one day, "What makes you cry?" He said, "I cry because I want a wife." Now his grandparents knew of a girl who lived toward the east and they sent him there.

As he went along the trail, he came to a giant's house. He went in to see the giant, who asked him to stay to breakfast. The giant had five roasts on the fire. He had four large roasts and one small one. He said to the boy, "Pick out the roast you want for breakfast." The boy picked out the small roast. Now, the four large roasts were the legs of people that the giant had killed. The small roast was venison. The boy knew this from what his grandmother had told him. She said, "Never eat too much."

After breakfast he went on. On the road he came to a great rock cliff. Its name was Cliff-Giant and it crushed people. The other giant had told him of this one, and how to get by it. He had said, "Turn yourself into a little dog and very slowly follow the trail under the Rock-Cliff. Keep your eye on Rock-Cliff. When you see it move, run fast." He did this and escaped. Then he went on.

He could see at a distance the place where the girl lived. Until he came in sight of this lodge he had never left off crying. Now, this girl had a great horse which would kill people before they could reach her lodge. That was her guard. The boy picked up two large stones and ran, still crying, toward the lodge. The animal ran at the boy, but the boy spat all over one of the stones. When the horse came close, he threw the stone behind him. Then the horse stopped to stamp on the stone and the boy ran on. He was almost in reach of the lodge when he threw the other stone. The horse stopped to stamp on that, and the boy reached the lodge and jumped in.

Very soon the girl entered. She knew him at once and called him by name — Iwapnep Ätswitki, Cry-because-he-had-no-wife. She talked to him and asked him if he wanted a bath. So she built a fire, heated water, and prepared him a bath. When he had taken the bath he became of man's size.

Next morning they started toward his home. When they reached this, his grandparents were very

CAYUSE SCOUT WHO WAS WITH McKAY AT THE CAPTURE OF THE MODOC
CHIEF, CAPTAIN JACK

Head dress is made chiefly of Modoc scalp locks taken at that time

Photo by Lee Moorhouse

LACK-UM-TIN, UMATILLA WARRIOR

The rawhide shield behind is ornamented with scalp lock and eagle feathers

old, because he had been gone many years. The girl said to her husband: "You tell your grandparents to do nothing wrong to-night. If they obey, I will give them a bath that will make them young again." In the morning she did so; but they had not obeyed her directions so they did not become young again. The next night they were both dead.

Then the girl and her husband started for her old home. They rode back on the great horse but he did not go very well. They made a whip out of black haw. The whip said to them, "I can outlast all other whips." They made a whip out of smoke-wood (Coyote-rope). This whip said, "When the giant gets too close, throw me down and I will tangle up the giant." They made a whip out of mud. This whip said, "Throw me down and I will mire the giant." They made a whip out of slide-rock. This whip said, "Throw me down and the giant will have trouble in getting by." They made a whip out of red haw. This whip said, "Throw me down, and I will tear the giant's flesh." They made a whip out of big mountains. This whip said, "Throw me down and the giant will not be able to get past me."

When they had finished all the whips, they started to pass the giant's house. The giant rushed out and cried, "Give me your wife!" The boy answered, "Get me a drink of water and I will give you my wife." When the giant went to get the water, the boy whipped up the horse and hurried on. They had gone some ways when the giant came out. They threw down the whip of black haw. He almost overtook them and they threw down the whip of smoke-wood. It tangled up the giant until they got away. When the giant almost overtook them again, they threw down the mud whip and he was mired. When the giant almost overtook them the fourth time, they threw down the slide-rock whip and the giant had great trouble in getting by. When the giant almost overtook them the fifth time, they threw down the red-haw whip, and it tore the flesh of the giant. And when the giant almost overtook them the sixth time, they threw down the whip of high mountains and he could not cross it. Thus they escaped.

HOW COYOTE GOT HIS CUNNING

Shastan

LONG, long ago, Chareya, Old Man Above, made first the fishes, then the lower animals. Afterwards he made a man. Chareya ordered the man to decide the rank of the animals. The man said he would give to each a bow. By the length of the bow given him would each animal know his rank. The next day, when the sun was new, would man give away the bows.

Coyote listened. If he received the longest bow, he would be the most important animal; he decided not to sleep. He would be the first one at the meeting place when the day was new.

Night Owl hooted, Wolf howled in the darkness, and Bat flitted over his head. Coyote slept not. Robin chirped and Thrush sang when the day was new. Coyote slept. So Coyote was last to reach the man and received the shortest bow of all. So Coyote became the meanest of all animals. But in his distress, Coyote howled to the man, and he, in turn, appealed to Old Man Above. Chareya ordered that Coyote should be the most cunning of all animals. And so he is to this day.

THE NAMING OF CREATION

Nez Percé

COYOTE was chief of all the animals. Now, he told them that the tribes of men were coming near, one and all. Everything he told them came true. Then he said, "To-morrow the people will come out of the ground. I will name them and they will spread out."

Then he named them; he named them until he had named them all. And the people came out, but Coyote had no name for himself. Many people came out. Then he named himself Coyote. Thus came people, — not we alone, but all people.

THE BIRD CHIEF

THEY called all the birds. They said, "The bird which, flying farthest, can reach the upper world, shall be chief." All the birds high in the air went to equal heights. Now Wren sat beneath the thick feathers of Eagle's wing. He sat there as Eagle flew.

The birds, all wing-tired, returned to earth. Only Eagle went above. When Eagle had gone as high as he could, Wren flew beyond him. When the birds had returned below, they waited. Eagle returned alone after a long time. They counted the birds. Behold! Wren only, he had not returned. They waited for him. At length, after a long time, he returned. Eagle was too highly thinking of himself, when behold, Wren was made chief.

THE SPELL OF THE LAUGHING RAVEN

Klamath

AT "dance place" when the Klamath Lake people danced, many people were there. Kemush, Old Man of the Ancients, went there. Then Old Raven laughed at them, laughed when they danced, and all people dancing there became rocks.

Gray Wolf entered Kitti above, from the north. There he stopped and lay down, although not yet having reached his home. In full dress, at that spot, moccasins with beads on toe, stopped and rested. Then Old Grizzly approached Old Gray Wolf while lying asleep. And Old Grizzly stole from Gray Wolf his moccasins, beads also, and put them on to go to the fishing place. Upon this, Old Gray Wolf, waking up, threw Old Grizzly down hill. He rolled him down over the rocks for having robbed him of moccasins and beads also. Thus killed he Old Grizzly.

Upon this, the Klamath Lake people began fighting the Northerners because Old Grizzly had been killed by Old Gray Wolf. Then Old Raven laughed at them when fighting and they became rocks.

CHILCAT BLANKET SHOWING EYE OF THE THUNDER BIRD

RAVEN WITH EYE OF THE THUNDER BIRD

ORIGIN OF THE THUNDER BIRD

LONG, long ago, Toe-oo-lux, South Wind, travelled to the north. There Toe-oo-lux met Quoots-hooi, the giantess. Toe-oo-lux said, " I am hungry. Give me something to eat."

Quoots-hooi said, " I have nothing to eat. You can get food by fishing."

So South Wind dragged the net. He caught tanas-eh-ko-le. He caught a little whale. South Wind took his stone knife to kill the whale.

Then the giantess said, " Use a sharp shell. Do not use your knife. Slit tanas-eh-ko-le down the back. Do not cut him crossways."

South Wind pretended not to hear. South Wind cut the whale across the back. Suddenly the fish changed into an immense bird. The bird's wings darkened the sun. The flapping of its wings shook the earth. This bird was the Thunder Bird. He flew to the north and lighted on Swal-al-a-host, near the mouth of Great River.

Then South Wind and the giantess travelled north to find him. One day, picking berries, Quoots-hooi found the nest of Thunder Bird. The nest was full of eggs.

Quoots-hooi broke one egg. It was not good, so she threw it down the mountain side. Before it reached the valley it became an Indian. Quoots-hooi threw down other eggs. Each egg became an Indian. That is how the Chehalis Indians were created.

Indians never cut the first salmon across the back. If they did, the salmon would not run. Always Indians slit the first salmon down the back.

MOUNT EDGECOMB, ALASKA

WHEN all the world was covered with rising waters, Chethl, Thunder, left his sister, Abhishanakhou, the Underground Woman. Chethl said, " Sister, you shall never see me again. You shall only hear my voice." He put on the skin of a great bird and flew away. His eyes flashed fire and the earth shook when he flapped his wings.

Abhishanakhou, the Underground Woman, climbed to the top of Mount Edgecomb. The top opened and she fell in, leaving a great hole. The world is an immense plate, resting on a tall pillar. The Underground Woman holds up the pillar so the plate will not fall. When storms break on Mount Edgecomb, the lightning from Chethl's eyes gleams through her crater windows. The flapping of his wings makes the plate tremble, and she hears the thundering of his voice. But she never sees Chethl.

AN INDIAN'S VOW TO THE THUNDER
GODS *

"TO an Indian woman the Thunder had spoken in a vision. To this god she promised to give her first-born child. When she became a mother, she forgot in her joy that the life of her little child did not belong to her; nor did she recall her fateful vow until one bright spring day when the clouds gathered, and she heard the roll of the Thunder,—a sound which summoned all persons consecrated to these gods to bring their offerings and to pay their vows. She remembered what she had promised, but her heart forbade her to lay the infant, which was smiling in her arms, upon the cloud-swept hilltop. She pressed the baby to her breast and waited in silence the passing of the gods in the storm. The following spring when the first thunder pealed, she did not forget her vow, but she could not gather strength to fulfil it.

* As related by Alice C. Fletcher. Used by permission. This incident is not a myth; it is actual fact. It is included because it throws light upon the softer side of Indian character, and because it shows also the extent to which the Indian was influenced by the religious beliefs which we term myths.

YAKIMA CHIEF

Scalp locks are here used as ornaments attached to the beaded yoke

PEO, CAYUSE WARRIOR

Another year passed and again the Thunder sounded. Taking the toddling child by the hand, the mother climbed the hill, and when the top was reached she placed it on the ground and fled. But the boy scrambled up and ran after her, and his frightened cry stayed her feet. He caught her garments and clung to them, and although the Thunder called, she could not obey; her vow had been made before she knew the strength of a mother's love. Gathering the boy within her arms, she hid herself and him from the presence of the gods. The storm passed, and the mother and child returned to the lodge, but fear had taken possession of her; she watched her son with eyes in which terror and love struggled for the mastery.

"One day as the little one played beside a rippling brook, laughing and singing in his glee, suddenly the clouds gathered, the flashing lightning sent beast and bird to cover, and drove the mother out to find her child. She heard his voice above the fury of the storm calling to her. As she neared the brook, a vivid flash blinded her eyes; for a moment she was stunned, but recovering, she pushed on, only to be appalled by the sight that met her gaze. Her boy lay dead, struck by the Thunder gods who had claimed their own.

"No other children came to lighten the sorrow of the lonely woman, but every spring when the first

Thunder sounded, and whenever the storm swept the land, this stricken mother climbed the hills, and there, standing alone, with hands uplifted to the black rolling clouds, she sang her song of sorrow and fealty.

"Many years ago the writer met her and heard her song; she was an old, old woman; she is now at rest and let us hope that her lifelong sorrow has turned to joy. The words of her song express her fidelity, and the music betrays her love and sorrow:

> " Flying, flying, sweeping, swirling,
>   They return, the Thunder gods.
>   To me they come, to me their own,
>   Me they behold, who am their own!
>   On wings they come, —
>   Flying, flying, sweeping, swirling,
>   They return, the Thunder gods."

CHINOOK GHOSTS

Chinook

THE ghosts wanted to buy a wife. They bought Blue Jay's sister, Ioi. They came in the evening and on the next morning Ioi had disappeared. Now Blue Jay was a wise bird, a foe to magic. After a year Blue Jay said, "I am going to search for Ioi."

Blue Jay asked all the trees, "Where do people go when they die?" They did not answer. Then Blue Jay asked all the birds, "Where do people go when they die?" They did not answer.

At last Blue Jay said to his wedge, "Where do people go when they die?"

Wedge said, "Pay me and I will tell you."

Blue Jay paid him, and Wedge took him on a journey. They arrived at a large village. The last lodge was very large. Smoke was rising only from this lodge. There Blue Jay found Ioi.

When Ioi saw Blue Jay, she said, "Where did you come from?"

Blue Jay said, "I am not dead. Wedge brought me here. Are you dead?"

Then Blue Jay opened all the lodges and he saw that they were full of bones. He saw a skull and bones close to Ioi. He said, "What are you going to do with that skull?"

Ioi said, "That is my husband."

When it grew dark, the bones became alive. Blue Jay asked, "Where did all these people come from?"

Ioi said, "Do you think they are people? They are ghosts."

After some time, Ioi said to him, "Go with those people fishing with a dip net."

He went with a young boy. The people spoke always in very low tones and he did not understand them. Ioi told him to speak in low tones. When they were going fishing in their canoe, another canoe came down the river. The people in it were singing. Blue Jay began to sing, too, and at once the boy became a skeleton. Blue Jay stopped singing and the boy became a ghost again. When Blue Jay spoke in loud tones, the boy always became a skeleton.

The ghosts caught leaves and branches in the dip net. These branches and leaves were their trout and salmon. Blue Jay shouted often and all the ghosts became skeletons.

One day when all the ghosts were bones, Blue Jay

changed their skulls. He put children's skulls on old people. Therefore the ghosts disliked him. They told Ioi to send him back. But he did not know in what to go. Their canoes were full of holes and covered with moss.

So Ioi sent Blue Jay home, but he did not follow her directions. Therefore he died and became a ghost. He returned to the ghost land and found all the bones were real men. The leaves and branches were real salmon and trout, and all their canoes were new.

THE MEMALOOSE ISLANDS

Klickitat

LONG ago, before the white man came, a young chief and a maiden loved one another. Suddenly the chief went over the spirit trail. But he could find no rest in the land of the spirits. The maiden also grieved for him. Then a vision came to the maiden. It told her to go to the land of the spirits.

The maiden told her father of the vision and they both obeyed. The father made ready a canoe, placed her in it and they paddled up Great River to the spirit island. Through the darkness, as they neared the death island, they heard singing and the tom-tom of the dance drum. Four spirit people met them on the shore. The maiden landed but the father returned. At the great dance house the maiden met her lover, more beautiful than on earth. All night long they danced. Then when morning came and the robins chirped, the dancers fell asleep.

The maiden slept, but not soundly. When the sun was high, she awoke. All around her were skeletons

MEMALOOSE ISLAND NEAR THE DALLES

The tombstone is that of Vic Trevett, a friend of the Indians, who showed their love for him by burying him in their sacred death island

A Scaffold Grave

and skulls. Her lover, with grinning teeth, was gazing upon her. The maiden was in the island of the dead. Struck with horror, she ran to the shore. At last she found an old boat and paddled herself across Great River to the Indian village.

But her father was frightened. She had been to the spirit land. Therefore, if she returned, evil would fall upon the tribe. That night again the father made ready a canoe and paddled across the river to the memaloose island. Through the darkness, they heard singing and the tom-tom of the dance drum.

In course of time a baby, half human, half spirit, was born. The spirit lover wished his mother to see it. He sent a messenger to her, telling her to come to the island by night. He told her, when she arrived, not to look at the baby until it was ten days old. After the old woman reached the memaloose island, she became impatient. She lifted the cloth from the baby's face. She lifted just one little corner and looked at the baby's face. Therefore the baby died. Thus the spirit people became displeased. They said that never again should living people visit the land of those who had gone by the spirit trail.

A VISITING GHOST

Teton

ONCE a young brave came to a great forest just at nightfall. He was alone, so he lay down at the edge of the woods. At midnight he heard a woman cry, "My son! my son!" Then he heard the breaking of twigs. Thus the warrior knew that some one was approaching. The warrior put brush on his fire, then he peeped through a hole in his blanket. A woman was approaching. She wore a skin dress with long fringe. She wore also a blanket drawn over her head. Her leggings were decorated with bead work and porcupine quills.

The woman came to where the warrior lay with his legs stretched out. She took his foot and raised it. Then she dropped it. Twice the woman did this. Then she drew a rusty knife.

The warrior sprang up.

He shouted, "What are you doing?"

Then he shot at her suddenly.

The woman ran away screaming, "Yun! yun! yun!"

When daylight came, the warrior saw he had camped near a scaffold grave. Therefore he said, "This is the ghost which came to me."

ORIGIN OF THE TRIBES

Chinook

LONG ago, in Lake Cle-el-lum, lived Wish-poosh, the monster beaver. Cle-el-lum was beautiful. It was also full of fish. The animal people wanted to fish there but Wishpoosh killed them. Wishpoosh dragged them into the water and drowned them. Wishpoosh also killed and ate the animal people.

At last Coyote tried to kill him. Coyote fastened a spear to his wrist with a strong cord. Then he began to fish in the lake. Soon Wishpoosh attacked him. Coyote speared the beaver. Then Wishpoosh plunged to the bottom of Cle-el-lum and dragged Coyote with him. But Coyote fought hard with Wishpoosh.

They fought so hard, they tore out the banks of Cle-el-lum. The waters rushed through the break, then through the mountains and down the cañon. They rushed into Kittitas Valley. The water formed another lake in Kittitas Valley.

Coyote and Wishpoosh fought so hard they tore out the banks of the new lake. The waters rushed

INDIAN TYPE. CHIEF JOSEPH OF THE NEZ PERCES

This tribe, except during the Nez Percé war, was always friendly to the whites

INDIAN TYPE. FISH-HAWK, PRESENT CHIEF OF THE CAYUSES
The Cayuse Indians were responsible for the Whitman massacre

down into the basin of the Cowiche, Nachess, and Atahnum. The water formed a larger lake. Yakima was flooded and a very great lake formed at Toppenish.

Coyote and Wishpoosh fought so hard that they tore out the banks of this very great lake. The waters rushed to the meeting-place of the Yakima, the Snake, and the Columbia Rivers. The waters here formed a very, very great lake.

Coyote and Wishpoosh fought so hard that even the banks of this lake were torn out. Then Wishpoosh dashed down the Great River. Coyote was out of breath. Coyote wanted to stop Wishpoosh. He caught at the trees and stones along the banks of Great River. Nothing could stop Wishpoosh. At last Coyote and the beaver reached the breakers at the mouth of Great River, reached the breakers of the Bitter Waters.

Wishpoosh was very angry. He killed salmon and swallowed them. He killed whales and swallowed them. Coyote saw that Wishpoosh was very strong. Then he remembered that he was Coyote, the wisest and cunningest of all the animals. So Coyote changed himself into a branch, a tree branch. He drifted toward Wishpoosh. Wishpoosh swallowed him. Then Coyote changed himself back into Coyote again. He took his stone knife. He cut the sinews inside of Wishpoosh. Thus Wishpoosh died.

Now Coyote was very tired. Therefore he asked Muskrat to help him. Together Coyote and Muskrat pulled the great beaver to land. Then they cut up Wishpoosh. They threw the pieces over the land.

From the head of Wishpoosh, Coyote made the Nez Percés, great in council. From the arms he made the Cayuses, powerful with the bow and war-club. From the legs he made the Klickitats, famous runners. From the ribs he made the Yakimas. From the belly he made the Chinooks, short, fat people, with big stomachs. Coyote at last had only the hair and blood of Wishpoosh. These he flung far up the valley to the east. They became the Snake River Indians, a tribe of war and blood.

Thus Coyote created the tribes. Then he returned up the Columbia.

Now in making the Chinooks and the coast tribes, Coyote forgot to give them any mouth. The god Ecahni, travelling along, noticed this. Then Ecahni called the tribes to him and with a stone knife gave each one a mouth. But for fun Ecahni cut them crooked. He made some mouths very big. Thus the coast tribes have not perfect mouths.

INDIAN TYPE. WHIRLWIND, MEDICINE MAN OF THE CAYUSES

TEPEE IN THE SAND AND SAGE BRUSH COUNTRY, EASTERN WASHINGTON

HOW THE OKANOGANS BECAME RED

Okanogan

LONG, long ago when the sun was young and no bigger than a star, there was an island far out at sea called Samahtumiwhoolah, or White Man's Island. Now giants lived there. The giants were white and their leader was a tall white woman, called Scomalt. At first there was peace, but at last war came and the white giants fought with each other. This made Scomalt angry. Scomalt had a strong heart. She drove the unruly ones together to the farthest end of the island. Then she broke off this piece of land and with her foot pushed it out to sea.

Many days drifted the floating island. Storms swept over them and the sun beat down upon them. At last all died except one man and one woman. Then the man caught a whale and they saved their lives by eating the blubber. Then their island began to sink, so they made a canoe. They put the blubber into the canoe and then paddled away.

After paddling for many suns, they came to some

islands, and at last to the mainland. Here they landed, but the mainland was not so large as it is now because it had not grown. But all their whiteness was gone. The sun had burned them until they were red. All the Okanogans are descended from this man and woman, and therefore they are red.

In time to come, the lakes will melt the foundations of the world and the rivers cut it loose. Then the whole world will float as the island did. This is the end of the world, the Itsowleigh.

THE COPPER CANOE

Nootka

LONG ago, from the waters of Whulge, a man came to the Nootkas. He came in a copper canoe, which shone bright as the sun. His paddles were also copper. Men said he came from the sky. He came to teach them they should not fight. At first the Nootkas listened, then they became angry. They killed the canoe man.

Indians were sorry after they killed the canoe man. Therefore they carve images of him for their houses, even to this day.

ORIGIN OF MINERAL SPRINGS

LONG, long ago, in the days of the first grandfather, all men were at peace. The earth was so new that tall firs of the mountain were no larger than arrows. Many fish swam in Beautiful Waters and in Great River. Many deer were on the mountains; many ipo and camas roots in the valley. All Indians were happy.

Then the first twins were born. One became famous for the deer he shot and the fish he speared. The other was always hungry. One day the brothers were hunting together. One leaned over the spring to drink. His brother struck him on the head with his stone tomahawk and pushed him into the spring. At once the water bubbled and boiled. From a cloud of vapor arose an old Indian. He was the first of all Indians. He said, "You have sharpened the tomahawk against your brother. Go. Wander. Wherever you drink, the waters shall be bitter."

The brother wandered over the mountains and plains. Wherever he drank the waters became bitter. For that reason Indians did not allow twins to live. One is always unlucky and the other happy.

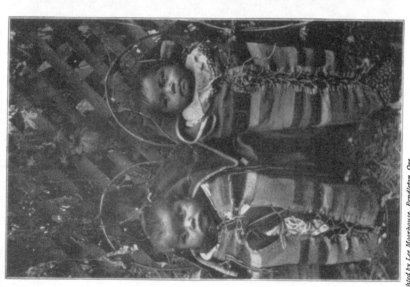

CAYUSE TWINS IN SUNSHINE AND STORM

AN INDIAN MOTHER AND PAPPOOSE

HOW THE ERMINE GOT ITS NECK-LACE

Athabascan

IN the valley between Koyukuk and Yukon lived an old man, his wife, and two sons. The old man was too feeble to go out alone any longer, so he told the boys they must travel alone. Therefore they decided to go alone.

In the morning they found a porcupine trail. Following this downstream, they came to a large river running full of ice. At the edge of the water the track disappeared. The brothers leaped on a cake of ice and floated downstream. Again they landed and looked for food, when they found a fish had been left on the ice, and saw many sled tracks. They followed these. They then heard a faint crying. Going on cautiously, they saw a porcupine carrying a load. They asked it why it cried. When it did not answer, they clubbed it dead, cooked it, and ate it.

Going on, they saw a village. An old woman came out, saw them, and called to the people of the village to prepare food for them. The brothers entered a large house, where an old man was seated on a caribou skin. They sat down on either side of him on caribou skins and began to eat. Seeing only young women, besides the old man and woman, the brothers asked where the young men were. The young women said there were none, but that they could do many difficult things which even men could hardly do. The elder brother boasted that he could do more than they. But the young women laughed. They said they were simply answering his question.

In the morning the young women went hunting. The brothers went with them. Then the women outran the elder brother and teased him. He became angry and said:

"You cannot do one thing. Stand at a distance and shoot at me. If I am not hit, I will shoot at you."

The younger man warned his brother; but the elder one was still angry and insisted. Finally the women consented to shoot at him. As they shot he leaped, but four arrows struck him together and he fell dead. The younger brother mourned for him.

When he wished to return and asked the way, he was told it was dangerous and they described to him

THE YUKON RIVER

The Yukon River in Winter

the monsters he would meet. Nevertheless he started.

After travelling for some time, he saw a cliff with a nest of enormous birds. The old ones were away, but he found a young eaglet.

"What do your parents do when they come?" he asked.

"When they come," the eaglet answered, "it becomes dark, it blows, and there is thunder. When it is my mother coming, it rains. When it is my father who comes, it hails."

The young man killed the bird. Then he waited. Soon it became dark, and thundered, and rained, while the air was blown against him by the beating of the wings of the Thunder bird. The young man shot it, and springing forward, killed it with his moose-horn club. When the other bird came, he killed it too.

He went on until he came to a porcupine as high as a hill, which lived in a cave. Through this cave the young man had to pass for he could find no way around it. Hiding outside the cave, he made a noise to attract the porcupine's attention. It at once started to back out, lashing its tail against the mountain side until the enormous quills were stuck all over the mountain and the tail itself was quite bare.

Then as it left the cave, the young man shot it and clubbed it to death.

Travelling on farther, he found the tracks of an enormous lynx. This the women had told him was the strongest of the monsters. Here, too, he tried to go around it but could not. Then he tried to shoot it, but the lynx caught the arrows in his claws. Seeing no way of escape, the young man gave up hope. Then the lynx ordered him to clear away the snow so that he could eat him more at ease, and to heap up the wood for the fire by which the young man was to be cooked. The young man did this, but the lynx told him to get still more firewood. The young man did this, going farther each time to get the wood. Soon he heard some one say:

"Brother, stand quickly on my back and I will carry you away."

"Where are you?" he asked.

"Here."

Looking down, he saw an ermine at his feet. He said, "I am afraid I will kill you if I step on your back."

"No, jump on me. I will carry you."

Then he jumped hard, but the ermine did not even move.

"Your back is too small. I cannot sit on it."

"Lay a stick across my back, and put another across my neck for your feet."

He laid the sticks across the ermine and sat down. Immediately it carried him to his house. The young man's parents were glad for his safe return. They gave the ermine a shell necklace.

COYOTE AND GRIZZLY

Nez Percé

ONCE there was a grizzly bear who was always angry. One day when travelling through the woods she came upon a band of Indians. She ate them all. In the evening, when she had reached home, she had a bad headache and in the night she became very sick because she had eaten so many Indians. She was sick for a week and almost died. She sent for Coyote to come as a medicine man. But Coyote said to his friends, "I do not care if she dies. It would not hurt me or anybody else. Everybody would be glad of it." But as his wife told him to go in company with others, he finally went to see Old Grizzly.

After a while he came to Old Grizzly's house and made medicine. Then she got well. He told her she was sick from eating too many choke cherries, because he thought all the people would run away if he told the truth and said it was from eating too many Indians. But when the people were gone and he himself was ready to run he told her she had eaten too many Indians.

Old Grizzly jumped up and chased Coyote. He

"OUT OF THE SMALL END OF THE STICK HE MADE FISHES"

(Page 34)

CAYUSE WARRIOR WITH TOMAHAWK AND TOM-TOM

ran up the hills; he ran down the valleys; he ran through the woods. At last he changed himself into a buffalo eating grass by the trail. Now Grizzly Bear thought she would catch Coyote, no matter into what form he changed himself. So when she saw the buffalo, she started to kill it, but then she saw Coyote's trail running past it. So she followed the trail. When she had gone some ways, Coyote changed himself into his own form again. He called after Grizzly Bear and said, " You are only a foolish old bear. You can never catch me."

When Grizzly Bear heard Coyote's voice, she started after him again.

After a while Coyote changed himself into an old man who had smallpox. He was in a tepee by the trail. His clothes were old and worn. When Grizzly Bear came up, she looked into the house. She asked the man if any one had passed. He told her a man had crossed the river. She saw a bridge with tracks on it. The bridge was made of willows. Now she thought she could get across on that bridge, so she walked on it. The bridge broke, she fell into the water, and was drowned.

Then Coyote turned himself into his own form and went back to his people. He told them he had killed Grizzly Bear.

COYOTE AND THE DRAGON

LONG ago, in the Willamette Valley, there lived a monster who made all the people afraid. It lived in a cave. At night it would come from its cave, seize and eat people, and return to the cave in the morning. All night it would eat the people. Coyote heard of this monster and decided to help the people. Coyote was the cunningest and shrewdest of all the animals.

Now the monster could not endure daylight. It lived always in the dark. So one day when the sun was very bright and high up in the heavens, Coyote took his bow and arrows and went to a mountain top. He shot one of the arrows into the sun. Then he shot another into the lower end of the first one, and then another into the lower end of the second. At last Coyote had a chain of arrows that reached from the sun to the earth. Then he pulled the sun down. He pulled hard until it came down. Then he hid it in the Willamette River.

Now the monster thought night had come. Everything was dark because the sun was hid in the river. So the monster came out from his cave and attacked the people. Then Coyote broke the chain which held the sun down, and it sprang up in the sky again. The monster was blinded because the light was so bright. Then Coyote killed it.

When the pale-faces found the big bones of the monster and carried them away, Indians said evil would come of it.

ORIGIN OF SPOKANE FALLS

Flathead

COYOTE and Fox were travelling together. They were coming up the river. When they got to where Spokane Falls now are, Coyote said to Fox: "I believe I'll get married. I'll take a woman of the Pend d'Oreilles for my wife."

So Coyote went to visit the chief of the Pend d'Oreilles. He said he wanted a wife.

Chief said, "No." Chief said that Pend d'Oreille women could not intermarry with other tribes.

Coyote said, "Then I will make a falls here in the river. I will make falls so that the salmon cannot get past them." That is how Spokane Falls were made.

UMATILLA WARRIOR WITH CEREMONIAL PIPE AND TOMAHAWK

Great Falls of the Missouri

COYOTE IN THE BUFFALO COUNTRY

Flathead

COYOTE took to the trail again. After a while he had nothing to eat. He was nearly starved. He went into a tepee at noon and lay down to rest. He was very weak because he had had nothing to eat. This happened in the Jocko Valley.

Coyote heard some one halloo, but he could not see any one. Then some one called again. After he had looked carefully for some time, Coyote saw Eagle a long ways off.

Eagle said that far away there was a country where there were buffalo all the time. Eagle said, "I am going there, but you cannot. You are too poor."

Then Coyote was angry. Coyote said, "I can go anywhere. I am going there." Coyote started out and in fifteen days he reached the place. It was near Great Falls. There was a big camp there and the chief's name was Bear. The people did not like Bear. When buffalo were killed, Bear would take the best pieces for himself — all the good meat and the chunks of fat.

Coyote wanted to be chief himself. So he killed a big buffalo and stripped off all the fat. Then he cut the meat in strips and hung it up to dry. After that he built a big fire and heated some stones red hot.

Bear heard that Coyote had killed a buffalo, so he came to look at the meat. Bear said, " This is nice meat. I will take it."

Coyote said, " I saved some fat for you."

Then Coyote took a red hot stone, wrapped it in fat, and put it in Bear's mouth. Thus Coyote killed Bear. Then the people made Coyote chief.

Now Bear was a great medicine man. Whatever he wished came true. There were many buffalo at Great Falls because Bear had wished it. After Coyote became chief all the buffalo went away. Then the people said, " Coyote is a bad chief."

Coyote went out again to hunt for buffalo. He was all alone and he hunted for five days. But the buffalo were all gone. Coyote was ashamed to go back to the camp so he kept right on.

In a little while Coyote met Wolf. Wolf said, " Where are you going ? "

Coyote said, " I am going to travel all over the world."

Wolf went on ahead. Soon Coyote heard some one coming. It was a man with plenty of meat. Coyote lay down by the trail and pretended to be dead. The man stopped. He said, " This is pretty good fur." So he threw Coyote among the meat and went on.

Coyote ate all the meat he could hold. Then he ran away. After a while he met Wolf again. Wolf said, " You look fat. Where did you get meat?"

Coyote told him he had pretended to be dead. He said, " The man wanted me for my fur. Your fur is finer than mine. If you pretend to be dead, you can get meat."

Wolf heard the man coming so he lay down by the trail and pretended to be dead. The man stopped. He said, " This is pretty good fur, but I 'll make sure he is dead." Then he hit Wolf with a club. He hit Wolf twice.

Then Wolf jumped up and ran away. Wolf was very angry. He said, " Coyote did this on purpose. I will kill Coyote."

Wolf ran and Coyote ran. After a while Wolf overtook Coyote. Wolf said, " Why did you play that trick on me. Now I will kill you."

Coyote said, " Wait until I tell you something. Then you can kill me."

Wolf said, " What do you want to tell me ? "

Coyote said, " There are only two of us. It is not fair for us to fight alone. Let us get others to fight with us. Then it will be like one tribe fighting another."

Wolf agreed. So Wolf went in one direction and Coyote in another. Wolf met Bear. Wolf said, " Come with me and fight Coyote." Then Bear and Wolf went on together.

In a little while they met Mole. Wolf said, " Come with me and fight Coyote." So Wolf and Bear and Mole went on together.

Now Coyote had gone in another direction. He met Cat and Dog. Coyote said, " Come with me and fight Wolf." So Coyote and Cat and Dog went on together.

Now Wolf reached the meeting-place first. He looked up and said, " I see Coyote coming." Coyote was coming with Cat and Dog. Coyote was dressed up, with beaded moccasins and a beaded shirt. Therefore he was a great chief. When the fight began, Coyote with Cat and Dog killed all his enemies. Then Coyote went on alone.

Photo by Lee Moorhouse

An Indian Home, Eastern Washington

Tepei and Salmon-Drying Scaffold

Photo by Lee Moorhouse

COYOTE AND THE SALMON

Klamath River

THEN Coyote went to Klamath River. He found the people very poor. They had no food. The river was full of salmon but the people could not get any. Three Skookums had built a dam to prevent the salmon from coming up the river. So the Skookums had all the fish, but the people had none. Coyote was very angry. Coyote said, " Before many suns, fish shall come up the river. The people shall have all the salmon they need."

Then Coyote went to the mouth of the river. The Skookums saw him. They thought he was only a skulking coyote. Coyote whined for some of their fish. Skookum would not give him any. Coyote came close to their camp. The Skookums drove him away. But Coyote saw where the Skookums kept the key of the dam. That was what he had wanted when he whined for fish.

Next morning, one Skookum started down to open the trap and let in a fish for herself. Coyote ran out of the tepee, jumped between Skookum's feet and tripped her up. Skookum fell and the key fell out of her hand. Then Coyote picked up the key, and went to the dam. Coyote opened the dam and let the fish through. The salmon went upstream into the country of the Cahrocs. Then the people had food to eat.

Afterwards Coyote broke down the dam. Ever since then salmon go every year up that river.

FALLS OF THE WILLAMETTE

TALLAPUS came from the coast to the Willamette Valley. Tallapus had been teaching the coast Indians. He found the Willamettes very poor and cold.

Now the Willamette was full of salmon, but the tribes were very stupid and feeble. They could not catch the salmon. So Tallapus made a tum-tum.* There the fish would come to the surface. Tallapus also made a trap. Tallapus began to make a tum-tum at Hanteuc. He did not like the place and left it. The gravel bar shows where he began to work. Then Tallapus went to Rock Island to make a tum-tum. Again he did not like the place and left it. The rapids show where he began to work. Then Tallapus began to make still another tum-tum. Here he liked the place and finished his work. White men call it the Falls of the Willamette. Here the salmon come to the surface in trying to leap over the falls. Then the stupid tribes could spear the salmon.

* "Tum" means "heart." Falls were named "tum-tums" because the sound of falling waters resembled, to the Indian, the beating of the heart.

At this tum-tum, Tallapus began to make a trap. Tallapus made one that would say "Noseepsk" when it was full. So Tallapus set the trap by the falls and began to make a fire. He began to rub the fire sticks together.

Then Trap called, "Noseepsk."

It was full of fine fish. Tallapus emptied it. He set the trap again by the falls and began to make a fire. He began again to rub the fire sticks together.

Then again Trap called, "Noseepsk! Noseepsk."

Tallapus emptied it. Then he set the trap again by the falls and began to make a fire. Before he could rub the fire sticks together, Trap called, "Noseepsk! Noseepsk!"

Then Tallapus was angry. He was very hungry and Trap would not let him make a fire. Tallapus said Trap should not call so soon.

Tallapus said, "Can you not wait catching fish until I build my fire?"

Then Trap was angry. Trap would not catch fish any more. Then the people had to spear the fish.

FALLS OF THE WILLAMETTE

Umatilla "The Place of Wind-drifted Sands"

TALLAPUS AND THE CEDAR

Clatsop

ONCE Tallapus was travelling from the country of the Tillimooks to the country of the Clatsops. Tallapus made himself a coyote.

Tallapus passed the mountains and headlands of the coast. Then he followed the trail through the deep woods. As he was travelling along, Tallapus saw an immense cedar. The inside was hollow. He could see it through a big gap which opened and closed. The gap opened and closed as the tree swayed in the wind. Tallapus cried, "Open, Cedar Tree!" Then the tree opened. Tallapus jumped inside. He said, "Shut, Cedar Tree!" Then the tree closed. Tallapus was shut inside the tree. After a while Tallapus said, "Open, Cedar Tree!" Then the tree opened. Tallapus stepped out of it. The tree was a very strange one. So Tallapus told the tree to open, and jumped inside. Then he told it to close. Tallapus did this many times.

At last Tallapus was inside the tree. Tallapus said,

"Open, Cedar Tree!" The tree did not answer. Tallapus was angry. He called to the tree. He kicked the tree. The tree did not answer. Then Tallapus remembered that he was Coyote, the wisest and cunningest of all animals. Then Tallapus began to think.

After he thought, Tallapus called the birds to help him. He told them to peck a hole through Cedar Tree. The first was Wren. Wren pecked and pecked at the great cedar until her bill was blunted. But Wren could not even make a dent. Therefore Tallapus called her Wren. Then Tallapus called the other birds. Sparrow came, Robin came, Finch came, but they could not even break the heavy bark. So Tallapus gave each a name and sent them away. Then Owl came, and Raven, and Hawk, and Eagle. They could not make even a little hole. So Tallapus gave each a name and sent them away. Then he called Little Woodpecker. Finally Little Woodpecker made a tiny hole. Then big Yellow Hammer came and pecked a large hole. But the hole was too small for Tallapus. So he saw there was no help from the birds.

Then Tallapus remembered again that he was Coyote, the wisest and cunningest of all the animals. Then Tallapus began to think.

After he thought, Tallapus began to take himself apart. He took himself apart and slipped each piece through Yellow Hammer's hole. First he slipped a leg through, then a paw, then his tail, then his ears, and his eyes, until he was through the hole, and outside the cedar tree. Then Tallapus began to put himself together. He put his legs and paws together, then his tail, his nose, his ears, then his body. At last Tallapus put himself together again except his eyes. He could not find his eyes. Raven had seen them on the ground. Raven had stolen them. So Tallapus, the Coyote, the wisest and cunningest of all animals was blind.

But Tallapus did not want the animals to know he was blind. Tallapus smelled a wild rose. He found the bush and picked two rose leaves. He put the rose leaves in place of his eyes. Then Tallapus travelled on, feeling his way along the trail.

Soon he met a squaw. Squaw began to jeer: "Oh, ho, you seem to be very blind."

"Oh, no," said Tallapus, "I am measuring the ground. I can see better than you can. I can see tomanowos rays." Squaw was greatly astonished. Tallapus pretended to see wonderful things at a great distance.

Squaw said, " I wish I could see tomanowos rays."

Tallapus said, " Change eyes with me. Then you can see tomanowos rays."

So Tallapus and Squaw traded eyes. Tallapus took Squaw's eyes and gave her the rose leaves. Then Tallapus could see as well as ever. Squaw could see nothing.

Tallapus said, " For your folly you must always be a snail. You must creep. You must feel your way on the ground."

Ever since that time snails have been blind. They have to creep slowly over the ground.

HOW COYOTE WAS KILLED

COYOTE had done many things. Fire he had stolen from Skookums and salmon he had given to the Indians. Therefore Coyote, thinking very highly of himself, wanted to travel to the sky world.

Now Star came every night very close to Coyote. Coyote lived above the clouds, on a mountain top. Therefore Coyote said to Star, "Take me with you." Star only laughed. Thus Coyote was angry. Coyote said every night when Star came, "Take me with you into the sky." But Star only laughed. Then Coyote howled at Star.

At last Star said, "To-morrow night I will take you to the sky world."

Next night Star came again to the mountain. Star came quite close to Coyote. Then Coyote leaped far and caught on the edge of Star. So they travelled through the sky world. Star climbed higher and higher. Coyote looked down. The tall firs of the forest were only as large as arrows. Then Coyote became cold, travelling high in the sky world. Star was not warm like Sun. Coyote became so cold he could not hold on. His paws slipped and he fell. Coyote fell far to the earth below him. For ten snows he fell. When Coyote struck the earth he was crushed as flat as a willow mat. Thus Coyote was killed.

OLD GRIZZLY AND OLD ANTELOPE

Klamath Lake Indians

OLD GRIZZLY lived with Old Antelope. Grizzly had two children. Antelope also had two children. One morning early they went to dig ipo roots, leaving their children at home. Old Antelope filled her basket before Old Grizzly had dug any ipo root. Old Grizzly kept on eating them up. Then they returned homeward. Again next day they went out to dig ipo, and again Old Antelope sooner filled her basket. Old Grizzly dug little. After their return they each gave ipo to their children. Then Old Grizzly thus enjoined her cubs:

"Ye shall not skip down from the lodge; the livers to ye would get loose. Ye shall not jump over the logs; ye would run against some sticks. Ye shall not dive under the water; smothering, ye might die."

Now again Old Grizzly next morning went again with Old Antelope to dig roots. Old Antelope soon filled the basket, Old Grizzly having dug little. Then Old Grizzly went to Old Antelope. She begged: " Insects bite me."

Old Antelope said, " A while from now I will bite you, when we have returned homeward."

Again Old Grizzly declared: " Insects bite me very hard in my fur."

After a while Old Antelope bit into the fur of Old Grizzly to kill the insects. Then Old Grizzly wanted also to bite into the fur of Old Antelope. Old Grizzly put ipo roots into her mouth. Crunching them, she pretended to bite insects, cracking them. Then she bit Old Antelope through the neck. She killed her in this manner, then cut her up wholly. All the ipo roots of Old Antelope she put in her basket, placing the meat on top. This she stuck on the top of a pole. A small portion of the meat she took home and gave to her children. Also to Old Antelope's children she gave meat.

The younger said, " But it tastes like our mother."

The elder pushed her: " Be silent. Say not so."

They saved the meat to eat until the next day.

Meanwhile Old Grizzly explained: " Your mother gave the Indians much meat, where she passed the night; but to me they gave only a little. To-morrow I shall go to look for your absent mother."

CELILO FALLS

Photo by Lee Moorhouse

THE DALLES

Photo by Lee Moorhouse

Early next morning Old Grizzly started out to fetch the meat. Then the young antelopes said to the grizzly cubs, "Let us skip down from the house."

Bear cubs said, "Our mother wants us not to skip down. Our livers might get loose."

Young antelopes again said, "Look here! We will jump over logs."

One cub said, "Our mother wants us not to jump over logs. We might run against tree limbs."

Again a young antelope said, "Look here! Let us dive."

The cub said, "Our mother wants us not to plunge in the water; smothering, we might die."

The young antelopes asked only once more, "Look here! Let us play 'smoke out.'"

The cub said, "Our mother told us not about this. Here we will play this."

The young antelopes threw rotten wood into the lodge, and went into it first. The bear cubs put the cover on. The young antelopes said, "Pretty soon you must open again."

"Yes," said the cubs.

Soon the young antelopes cried: "Two smoke in, two smoke out; two smoke in, two smoke out, . . .

smother, smother; oh! oh!" Then the cubs opened
the cover. The young antelopes went out.

Then the cubs went in, saying, "Pretty soon ye
must uncover."

"Yes," said the young antelopes.

The cubs cried: "Smoke in, smoke out; smoke
in, . . . smother, smother!"

Again the young antelopes went into the lodge.
"Two smoke in, two smoke out, . . . smoke,
smoke!" The cubs uncovered and the antelopes
came out.

The cubs again ran into the lodge. "Two smoke
in, two smoke out, . . . smother, smother!" This
time the young antelopes would not uncover for the
cubs.

After their death the young antelopes uncovered
the lodge. Then taking out the cubs, red paint
they lined in their faces. Gagging the nose of the
elder, they lifted it up to the top of the lodge.
Gagging the mouth of the younger, they fastened
it on the lodge ladder. Then they went into the
fireplace. Every article they enjoined not to report
to Old Grizzly when she returned. The bone awl
alone they forgot as it stuck in the roof.

After a while Old Grizzly returned, being ahead
of herself. Angered at their having wasted red paint,

she said, "They have wasted my red paint which I stole from the Indians. Then approaching nearer she saw the cubs to be dead. Sobbing, she said, "Now the children of Old Antelope have punished me."

To the young antelopes she called, "Where are ye, children?"

The children replied to Old Grizzly: "Right here we are, sitting in the sunshine."

Old Grizzly ran out to where now the children were sitting. But again the children spoke toward the mud house in reply to Old Grizzly. Again Old Grizzly ran into it.

"Children!"

Again the young antelopes replied to Old Grizzly: "Here we play, out of doors. You do not find us."

Grizzly thought it was the voices of the children. But the articles enjoined by the children had done as they had been told, and had answered her.

But after some time, the bone awl Shakta, which had stuck in the ceiling and had been forgotten, said, "Long ago the children whom you look for went away."

Old Grizzly said, "Which way, then, travelled they?"

And the awl Shakta told Grizzly: "Through

here they crawled; and here they placed coals against the opening."

Then Old Grizzly attempted to crawl through the hole, to follow the children. She could not crawl through. Finally she broke through and went on her way crying : "Rotten wood, rotten wood breaks easily. Rotten wood, rotten wood breaks through." Walking, Old Grizzly wept thus. Then she said, "Where are ye? I am going to find the children." She said this repeatedly while walking.

Finally she overtook the young antelopes while they camped in a cave, but she did not see them. Building a large fire she lay down. Now the children became aware that Old Grizzly had overtaken them ; and the elder antelope woke up the younger one.

"Now she has caught up with us," she said to the younger, and woke up the little one.

Old Grizzly went to sleep lying near the fire. "To-morrow at last I will play a game with ye children in daytime, seeing more sharply then." So speaking and lying down she went to sleep.

Then the young antelopes threw sticks at the sleeping one. They threw them to try whether she was asleep. But she not moving, they ran out of the cave at a quick pace.

ALASKAN BASKETS

KLICKITAT BASKETS

Afraid that Old Grizzly might overtake them, they hallooed to Old Crane, Shukamtchash, who, fishing minnows, skirted the water. "Cross us over, uncle, very fast. She is chasing us and will overtake us now." Old Crane crossed them over. The young antelopes explained to Old Crane. Then Old Crane blew them into a whistle stick and hung them up in the lodge, but they rattled for fear. At the message of the young antelopes that Old Antelope was killed by Old Grizzly, Old Crane and the young ones, too, wept.

Old Crane wept, crying, "Lake water, lake water."

The young cranes also wept, crying, "Lake wa-wa-water."

Now Old Grizzly, awakening after a time, looked around the cave. "I shall play a rather hard game with the children in the daytime, when able to see better. Long ago, after they left the cave, they reached Old Crane's home." So Old Grizzly started to follow the young antelopes; the tracks of them she followed.

Reaching the river, she asked Old Crane, "Have you seen the children?"

Old Crane said, "Not I saw the children."

Yet here were the out-going tracks of the children having reached there.

So Old Grizzly hallooed: "You want to conceal them then. Set me over quickly."

Old Crane said, "I have no canoe."

Again said Old Grizzly, "Quickly cross me over; fast set me over."

After a while Old Crane spread out his legs, one leg carrying a drinking cup, and let Old Grizzly use it as a bridge. Old Grizzly stepped on his leg. Coming to the midst of the river, she drank water from the drinking cup. And to shake out the water, after drinking, she struck Old Crane's leg with the drinking cup. Old Crane, angered, doused Old Grizzly into the water. Then fetching a bow from home, Old Crane shot Old Grizzly. Then the young antelopes came out of the whistle. With bows and arrows borrowed from the Crane children, they shot Old Grizzly. Thus they killed her.

LEGEND OF THE KLICKITAT BASKET

Klickitat

SHADE told the first weaver to weave tooksi, the basket. Weaver said, "I do not know how." But she went to the forest. She thought for a long time how to weave tooksi. Then she gathered the plant yi, with squaw grass, elk grass, pine grass, and noo-wi-ash, the red cedar roots. Then Weaver began to work. She worked very hard for many days. Then tooksi, the basket, was finished. Weaver carried it to the lake. She dipped it full of water, but the water leaked out.

Shade said, "It will not do. Weave again. Weave a tight basket with a pattern in it." Weaver was very sorrowful. Weaver sat by the lake mourning. At last, in the clear water, Weaver saw the pattern, chato-timus. Then Weaver was happy again.

She went again into the deep forest and pulled up noo-wi-ash, the red cedar roots. Then Weaver began to work. She worked very hard for many days. Then tooksi, the basket, was finished. Weaver carried it to the lake. She dipped it full of water. This time the water did not leak out. The basket was tight and it had a pattern on it, as Shade had told her. Other weavers learned the pattern. Thus the Klickitats have plenty of baskets. They do not leak and they have a pattern in them.

THE NORTHERN LIGHTS

Wabanski

"OLD CHIEF M'SARTTO, Morning Star, had one son only, so different from other boys of the tribe as to be worry to Old Chief. He would not stay and play with the others, but would take his bow and arrows and leave home for days at a time, always going toward the North. When he come home, they say, ' Where you been ? What you see ? ' But he say nothing.

"At last Old Chief say his wife, ' That boy must be watched. I will follow him.'

"So next time Chief M'Sartto kept in his trail and travel for long time. Suddenly his eyes close an' he could not hear. He had a curious feeling, then know nothing. By'm-by his eyes open in a queer light country, no sun, no moon, no stars, but country all lighted by strange light. He saw many beings, but all different from his people. They gather 'round and try to talk, but he not understand their language. M'Sartto did not know where to go or what to do. He well treated by this

strange tribe. He watch their games and was
'tracted to wonderful game of ball he never saw
before. It seemed to turn the light to many colors
and players all had lights on their heads and all wore
very curious belts called Menquan, or Rainbow belts.

"In few days an old man came and speak to
M'Sartto in his own language and ask him if he
know where he was.

"Old Chief say, 'No.'

"Then old man say, 'You are in country of
Wa-ba-ban, Northern Lights. I came here many
years ago. I was the only one here from the
" Lower Country " as we call it; but now there is
a boy comes to visit us every few days.'

"Then M'Sartto asked how old man got there,
what way he come.

"Old man say, 'I follow path called Spirits' Path,
Ket-a-gus-wowt, — Milky Way.'

"'This must be path I come,' said Old Chief.
'Did you have queer feeling as if you lost all knowl-
edge when you travelled?'

"'Yes,' say old man, 'I could not hear or see.'

"Then say M'Sartto, 'We did come by same
path. Can you tell me how I get home again?'

"'Yes, Chief of Wa-ba-ban will send you home
safe.'

"'Well, can you tell me where I can see my boy?—the boy that comes here to visit you is mine.'

"Then old man tell M'Sartto, 'You will see him playing ball if you watch.'

"Chief M'Sartto very glad to hear this, and when man went round to tepees telling all to go have ball game, M'Sartto went too. When game began he saw many beautiful colors.

"Old man ask him, 'Do you see your boy there?'

"Old Chief said he did. 'The one with the brightest light is my son.'

"Then they went to Chief of Northern Lights, and old man said, 'Chief of Lower Country wants to go home and also wants his boy.'

"So Chief of Northern Lights calls his people together to bid good-bye to M'Sartto and his son; then ordered two K'che Sippe, Great Birds, to carry them home. When they went travelling Milky Way he felt the same strange way he did when going and when he came to his sense he found himself near home. His wife very glad he come, for when boy told her his father was safe she pay no notice, as she afraid M'Sartto was lost."

THE END